LIFE IN
NORMAN ENGLAND

Life in
NORMAN
ENGLAND

O. G. TOMKEIEFF

English Life Series
Edited by PETER QUENNELL

CAPRICORN BOOKS • NEW YORK

To Serge and Michael

First published 1966
© O. G. Tomkeieff, 1966
CAPRICORN BOOKS EDITION 1967
Published by arrangement with
B. T. Batsford Ltd., London

Second Impression

Preface

A complicated jigsaw puzzle with a number of missing pieces, some of them vital links in the formation of the picture—this metaphor might be applied, not unjustifiably, to 'Life in Norman England'. The preceding period is, in some respects, better off, because the language of court and people was the same and there was a secular literature in the vernacular. The succeeding periods are obviously better off, with the revival of the English language and the beginning of a whole range of official documents about the year 1200, when record keeping can be said to have begun.

Medieval scholars have been, and are, working busily to fill in the blanks in the picture of Norman England. It is certain that they will never be completely successful. Some material was never recorded and many records have been lost, as there was no attempt to preserve them. This means that controversy rages over the interpretation of points which are not fully documented, and that conjecture must help to fill in the gaps in our knowledge. In a book of this size it is impossible to enter into controversy or to mention all the different interpretations which have been put forward. Some generalisation is essential and generalisation must always obliterate the finer shades of meaning and of argument. In such circumstances I have done my best to steer clear of the most controversial topics and, where that has not been possible, to follow majority opinion. I hope also that the reader will be able to distinguish in my writing between established fact and what must needs be conjecture.

The 'village Hampden' of Gray's Elegy in the eighteenth century was totally unsung in the eleventh and twelfth. We rely on odd scraps of incidental information, eked out by facts known from earlier and later times. In our period, more than in any other, we depend on ecclesiastical writing and, still more, on ecclesiastical illumination. But biblical characters and national saints, appearing in books written or copied in the eleventh and twelfth centuries, wear the dress of those centuries and live, eat and fight according to their customs. They can, therefore, if we ignore the occasional haloes and wings, illustrate accurately life in Norman England.

I have made no attempt to work out the values of medieval coins in terms of our own money. There was considerable inflation in the course of the Norman period, and the galloping inflation of today makes any standard of comparison impossible. I can only say, as I have said in the text, that 30 pence would buy an ox for the first half-century or more and that 5s. a day and his keep was a princely salary for Henry I's Chancellor. These two facts can be used as criteria for assessing approximately the value, in terms of modern money, of the wages and prices quoted in the book.

Individual acknowledgement of my debt to the many specialists on whose work I have drawn for my material is unfortunately impossible here. Some of their books, together with books of a more general nature, appear in the lists of books for further reading given at the end of each chapter. I would, however, like to express my particular thanks to two friends and sometime colleagues. Professor G. W. S. Barrow read my typescript and was able to warn me in time of two errors which had crept into my text. Mrs D. W. Delacourcelle examined the book from the point of view of the general reader and I owe her a very great debt for her most helpful comments and criticisms.

Newcastle upon Tyne   O. G. T.

Contents

The Illustrations

Note The first illustration from a British Museum manuscript is acknowledged in full; thereafter the reference has been shortened and the abbreviation 'B.M.' used.

viii

THE ILLUSTRATIONS

ix

THE ILLUSTRATIONS

xi

Acknowledgement

The author and publishers wish to thank the following for permission to reproduce the illustrations appearing in this book:

Aerofilms and Aero Pictorial Ltd for pages 36 and 93; Hallam Ashley, F.R.P.S. for page 37; the Ashmolean Museum, Oxford for page 19; the Bodleian Library, Oxford for pages 114 and 169; the Trustees of the British Museum for pages 6, 7, 9, 10 (bottom), 11, 14 (bottom), 16 (both), 17, 20, 27, 43, 49 (bottom), 60 (bottom), 65 (bottom), 73, 85, 89, 91, 94, 101, 103, 117, 118, 119, 122 (top), 125, 137 (both), 141, 145, 148, 155, 165 (both), 166 (both), 167 (top) and 168; Dean and Chapter of Canterbury Cathedral for page 157; the Master and Fellows of Corpus Christi College, Cambridge for the frontispiece and pages 45, 67, 69, 84, 102, 113 and 123 (bottom); the Courtauld Institute for the frontispiece and pages 45, 67, 69, 96 and 102; G. C. Druce for page 147 (bottom); the Chapter of Durham Cathedral for pages 50, 92, 109 and 121; Herbert Felton, F.R.P.S. for page 151; *Illustrated London News* for page 64; A. F. Kersting, F.R.P.S. for pages 31, 52, 78, 135, 140, 142 (bottom), 153 and 160; King's Lynn Archaeological Survey and Mrs Helen Parker for page 75; Quentin Lloyd for page 65 (top); Mansell Collection for page 97; Ministry of Public Building and Works (Crown copyright reserved) for page 33; National Buildings Record for pages 22, 24, 134 and 144 (both); Newcastle University for page 31; Oxford University Press and A. L. Poole for page 71; the Master and Fellows of Pembroke College, Cambridge for page 96; Royal Commission on Historical Monuments (Crown copyright reserved) for pages 34, 52 and 159; Dr J. K. St Joseph for pages 12 and 68, and (Crown copyright reserved) pages 8, 18 and 72; Edwin Smith for page 98; the Controller of H.M. Stationery Office (Crown copyright reserved) for pages 30 (top) and 57; the Master and Fellows of Trinity College, Cambridge for pages 38, 51 (bottom), 111, 122 (bottom), 123 (top), 128 and 147 (top); the Board of Trinity College, Dublin for page

ACKNOWLEDGEMENT

138 (bottom); E. W. Tristram for pages 161 and 162; the Master and Fellows of University College, Oxford for page 169; the Trustees of the Victoria and Albert Museum (Crown copyright reserved) for pages 143, 156 and 164; the Warburg Institute for pages 14 (top), 129 and 164.

The illustration on page 30 is reproduced from *The History of the King's Works*, *Vol. 1* (H.M.S.O.) and those on pages 161–2 from E. W. Tristram *English Medieval Wall Painting: the Twelfth Century*.

Thanks are also due to the following publishers for permission to quote from various edited and translated works: to Jonathan Cape, Ltd for the quotations on pages 94 and 95 from *The Autobiography of Gerald of Wales* (tr. M. E. Butler); to Constable & Co., Ltd for the two verses on page 168 from Helen Waddell *Medieval Latin Lyrics*; to the Cymmrodorion Society for the quotation on page 39 from Walter Map *De Nugis Curialium* (tr. M. R. James; Cymmrodorion Record Series, No. 9); to the Historical Association for the quotation on page 85, translated by H. E. Butler, from F. M. Stenton *Norman London*; to Thomas Nelson & Sons, Ltd for the quotations from their 'Medieval Texts', on page 42 from *Constitutio Domus Regis*, a supplement to *Dialogus de Scaccario* (ed. and tr. Charles Johnson), and on page 59 from *Chronicle of Jocelin of Brakelond* (ed. M. E. Butler); to the Oxford University Press for the quotations on pages 148 and 149–50 from L. F. Salzman *Building in England down to 1540*.

xiv

Introduction

The period selected for this particular volume cannot be precisely defined in years. Approximately, it runs from the accession of Edward the Confessor in 1042 to the early years of the thirteenth century. A more obvious starting point would be 1066, the Norman Conquest, but as one purpose of the book is to examine the effect of the Conquest on the lives and destinies of the people of England, it has been necessary to look at English society before the débâcle. The Norman period ends in 1154. We include also the early Angevins, Henry II and his sons, Richard and John. There are several factors which combine to give this period an historical unity. In the first place the accession of Edward the Confessor, half Norman by birth and wholly Norman by upbringing, marks the beginning of Norman influence in England and of a connection between England and Normandy, which was not severed until the loss of Normandy by John in 1204. For 100 of the 162 years of this period Normandy and England were linked, and linked so closely that their officials were interchangeable, their barons were the same on both sides of the Channel and men could pay their taxes in either Normandy or England. For half of those 100 years (1154–1204) the men who were the kings of England were lords of the whole of western France, a far greater area than that directly controlled by the French kings. This does not mean that England ruled French territory. On the contrary, it means that the rulers of Normandy and western France ruled England, French-speaking kings with a French-speaking aristocracy.

1

Such a state of affairs could hardly fail to leave its impress on life in England. Moreover, the actual timing of this continental connection was important. The preliminaries, as it were, of the great Twelfth-Century Renaissance date back to approximately the middle of the eleventh century. That very expansionism, which drove the Normans abroad to found kingdoms in England and southern Italy and to anticipate the Crusades in their efforts to drive the Moslems out of Spain, an expansionism which was to be seen in the rallying of most of western Europe to the crusading call of Pope Urban II in 1095, was both cause and effect of the spirit of enquiry and intellectual adventure which was the Twelfth-Century Renaissance. The main centres of this Renaissance were northern France and northern Italy and the identity of England with parts of northern France at this period meant that she shared in the great adventure.

In 1016 England had been conquered by the Danish Cnut and was ruled by him and his two sons until 1042. It was when Harthacnut died childless in that year that the first crisis in the English succession arose. Cnut's Danish kindred had a possible claim and so had the King of Norway, because in the Treaty of the Elf it had been agreed that, if either died without heirs, the other should succeed. However, there was a candidate with more claim to the loyalty of England than either of these. Edward, son of Ethelred II and his Norman wife Emma, had been living in exile at the Norman court during the Danish interlude. He was now recalled to the throne of his ancestors. For much of his reign of 23 years Edward was under the domination first of Earl Godwin, whose daughter Edith he married, and then of Harold Godwinson. Certain Norman elements did, however, creep into English life. There were Norman prelates, for a few years a Norman Archbishop of Canterbury, a Norman abbot and other Normans scattered about the country, in particular a Norman colony in Herefordshire on the Welsh border, followers of a Norman cousin of Edward, who made him Earl of Hereford. It was here that the first Norman-type castles were raised.

Duke William's victory in 1066 not only won him a crown and a tremendous accession of wealth, but it once more linked England's destinies with those of the Latin west. William

2

himself was not lacking in appreciation of what he had acquired. England was not a nation of barbarians overrun by the civilised Normans. What evidence we have suggests the contrary—that in most of the arts of peace the English were ahead of their conquerors. Certainly the English kingship was better organised than the dukedom of Normandy or the kingdom of France, and it seems clear that William, who claimed the crown as the designated heir of Edward and the elect of the English Witan, would have liked to retain as much as possible of the English system and of the personnel to work it. Two things worked against this hope. In the first six years of the reign constant rebellion cut down by death and voluntary exile the number of Englishmen of rank and, on the other hand, William's invasion of England was not carried out by an army under obligation to follow him. Apart from a certain number of mercenaries, the 6,000 or so who made up William's forces at Hastings were in the adventure for what they could get out of it. William had to reward his followers with confiscated lands, and these followers, mostly Norman but including Bretons and Flemings, could not fail to reproduce on English soil the customs and the way of life and even the language they had always known, especially as most of them, being already landowners on the Continent, divided their time and energies and were as much at home in Normandy as in England—until the final split in 1204.

William, therefore, introduced an alien aristocracy, an alien military caste into England, while retaining as much as possible of the Anglo-Saxon inheritance. He brought feudalism as it was known on the Continent. In ecclesiastical as in lay spheres he introduced a new, continental personnel into the higher ranks and brought the Church into line with the new reform movements on the Continent. At the same time he spread his feudal net to include church dignitaries as well as lay barons. For at least one generation after the Conquest these new arrivals were hated intruders, who lived uneasily on their new estates and must always be prepared to defend their lives and property; hence the castles which sprang up like mushrooms over the whole of England; hence also the famous 'murder fine' by which William sought to protect his followers. If a murdered man could not be proved to be an Englishman, the neighbourhood in which the body was found must either produce the murderer or pay a heavy fine. Like so many of our English laws this particular one outlived its function and was a useful way of collecting fines for the royal exchequer when, as the author of the *Dialogus de Scaccario* wrote at the end of the twelfth century, it was almost impossible to distinguish Norman from English.

The twelfth century was the period when the two races were settling down together, although this applied more to the lower classes and to the new 'bright boys' from the ranks, who were coming to the fore, than to the higher ranks of the feudal hierarchy. Norman French was still the language of the court. The king still, except for Stephen, spent much of his time and energy on the Continent and so did his barons. For Henry II and for Richard I England was something of a side-show. Henry II spent exactly one-third of his 35 years' reign in this country and Richard only six months of a ten years' reign. The loss of Normandy, Maine, Anjou and Touraine in the early years of the thirteenth century, and the refusal of Philip II of France to accept as his tenants for French lands men who also held land in England, meant that families with lands on both sides of the Channel had to split into French and English branches. For the first time since 1066 the ruling class in England had perforce to become English. The first fruits of this was Magna Carta, 1215, but the full effects were to appear in the reign of Henry III (1216–72) and later, when the English tongue, enriched by French words, was to come into its own, with a literature which was to reach its peak with Chaucer and Langland in the fourteenth century. Once again, too, England became an island and developed as islands are wont to do, in its own individual way. But these things do not concern us in this book, which treats of life in England when it belonged to the European community.

I

Prelude to the Norman Conquest

The England of Edward the Confessor covered much the same area as today. The peoples who inhabited the realm were, however, of no uniform breed and the differences showed then, as indeed they still do to a much lesser extent, in language and custom. The northern area, covering Northumberland and Durham, was an unconquered, isolated outpost of the old Anglian settlements, and was closely akin to the Anglian province between Northumberland and the Forth, which politically belonged to Scotland. There were a few Scandinavian infiltrations through the Tyne Gap from Norwegian settlements in the Isle of Man and Cumberland. These are shown mainly in place-names—the fells, the haughs, the thwaites, etc. Most of Cumberland and Westmorland at this time was racially and politically in Scotland. South of the Tees the modern Yorkshire, which then included part of Westmorland and south Cumberland, was Danish in character, in speech and in custom, and there was a strong attraction between it and the Danish homeland. South of the Humber and east of the Roman Watling Street was also predominantly Danish, though less strongly so in the region of the Wash and East Anglia than in the Trent valley. One characteristic of this 'Danelaw' was that it counted in multiples of six instead of five and that its 100 was a 'long hundred' of 120. Another and more important difference was that the Danish pirates and adventurers who settled in these areas had managed

*Peasant talking to group of his betters
(note puttee-like hose and long back-hair)*

to maintain their freedom and independence to a greater extent than their English neighbours in the south and west, who had suffered for a century from Danish raids. Of the non-Danish areas, Kent was the most prosperous region, in part because of its accessibility to the Continent. Cornwall was, and has remained, racially different. It was incorporated but not settled by the Saxons. So the England of Edward the Confessor was not a unity.

Physically it was a very different country from the one we know today. Forest and marsh and wild moorland would have been repeated to the point of monotony could a twentieth-century airman have surveyed early eleventh-century England. Populated areas must have been well scattered. The population of the whole country was probably about one-and-a-half million, and of this meagre total a large proportion was to be found in the coastal strip between the Humber and the Thames. About 10 per cent inhabited what were known as boroughs, London being outstanding with a population of more than 10,000, housed within the old Roman walls and giving a population density of about 60 to an acre. For the rest, York, Lincoln and Norwich could boast some 1,000 houses each, i.e. probably about 6,000–7,000 inhabitants. Oxford, Thetford and Ipswich had about 800 houses each, or some 5,000 inhabitants, and the smallest boroughs might count not more than 1,000 heads each. The rest of the population lived in small villages or hamlets or in isolated houses established in some hard-won forest clearing. Pre-1066 England was therefore predominantly rural and even the boroughs, even London, had fields and meadows, and their business life was governed to a greater or lesser degree by the demands of the agricultural year.

6

In fact the smaller towns existed as markets for the disposal of any surplus agricultural produce of the immediate neighbourhood and the supply, in many cases by merchants resembling travelling pedlars, of what might be called luxury goods, to be bought by those who had agricultural surplus to sell.

This would probably not be the ordinary peasant, although 'peasant' is a word we should not use before the Norman Conquest. The French '*paysan*' literally means 'countryman'. The Anglo-Saxon equivalent was '*gebur*', which has left its mark on the English language as boor and boorish. We have two accounts, written probably about 1050, describing the work done on an estate and the part played by the various people living there. The more important of these two documents is called the *Rectitudines Singularum Personarum* (the Rules of Individual People) and it seems to have been written for the guidance of the steward—the land agent. It contains a most valuable description of the rights and duties of the various people who combine to form an agricultural community, from the man we would call a yeoman farmer to the various herdsmen, both free and slave (for slaves there were in pre-Conquest England). The writer warns us: 'The customs of estates are various. Nor do we apply these regulations, which we have described, to all districts.' This is a salutary warning, for it is almost true to say that no two villages were alike. Some would consist of men working

Smith at work, watched by women (note head drapery)

A street village: Appleton-le-Moors, Yorkshire, showing modern successors of medieval crofts, with approach roads to fields behind them

together to carry out agricultural routine in the type of village which prevailed wherever in England the physical conditions permitted—the village with its dwellings stretched out along a track or surrounding a green, each with its small enclosure for domestic fowls, pigs, etc. and possibly some vegetables, and with the fields, meadows, woodland and uncultivated waste spreading out beyond the inhabited area.

Over many of these villages from an early time one or more of the king's followers, *thegns*, would have obtained rights, which would probably include food-rents or contributions towards his maintenance. In the course of centuries, bad harvests, bad farming, bad luck, or, worse still, the devastating effects of the Danish invasions of the ninth century, had made these near-subsistence farmers dependent upon the local 'squire'. He would provide 'for each rood of land, two oxen, one cow, six sheep and seven acres sown, together with tools for his work and utensils for his house. When death befalls him let the lord take charge of what he leaves.' This farmer was personally free. His blood price, if he was killed, was 200 West Saxon shillings. He paid local taxes and helped to maintain the church. Whether the land he farmed was his own or whether he was a rent-paying tenant he

8

must work for his lord, on some estates two days a week, on others three, with extra—or boon—works at seed-time and harvest, and contributions to the lord's larder in the form of barley and beans, sheep at Easter and tenpence for tribute or rent. These services and contributions in kind were a substitute for a higher tribute, which could not be paid in any other way at a time when the coinage in circulation was inadequate and labour not fluid enough for free hire. While a substantial proportion of the inhabitants of a village would be men of this 'income group', there might be others (*geneats*) with more land and higher status who, in lieu of rent, also owed services to their lord, but these services had a less degrading flavour. They were escort services, guard services and services connected with sport.

Then there were the poorer villagers, 'cottars' or cottagers, who had very little arable land—the average was five acres—and who owed one day's work a week in return for it. Each of these tenements, large or small, was held not by a single individual but by a family, and it was this which made the system workable. While one member of the family was doing the allotted number of days' work on the lord's land, the others could be cultivating the family holding. If the family was too large, the extra members would form a reserve of labour for the craftsmen's jobs necessary in a village, those of the carpenter and the smith, and also for the odd jobs of the agricultural world, those of the shepherd, swineherd, cowherd, beekeeper and the like. It was only at peak periods, like harvest time, that the whole

Shepherds

Reaping barley with a sickle

family, except the housewife, was expected to serve. Of course, this would mean the postponement of the villager's own harvesting, but this was not a reason for unmitigated gloom. In fact the mitigation is stated by the author of the *Rectitudines*. 'There are many common rights: in some districts are due winter provisions, Easter provisions, a harvest feast for reaping the corn, a drinking feast for ploughing, food for making the rick, at wood-carrying a log from each load, at corn-carrying food on completion of the rick, and many things which I cannot recount.' In other words the dull routine and the meagre, monotonous diet of the villagers might be enlivened by feasting at the lord's expense, and the occasional perquisites helped to see them through the year. These seasonal get-togethers were also occasions for jollification. For instance, November seems to have been the traditional month for wood-carrying and in addition to the free logs the workers seem to have got a free bonfire, centuries before Guy Fawkes gave his name to the modern edition of an ancient custom.

All these villagers were legally free men, whose freedom was limited in varying degrees by their economic dependence on a landowner. But many of the landowners, and even certain of

November bonfire

Threshing and winnowing

the richer villagers, particularly in Kent, actually owned men, women and children. Slavery was accepted. The slave was a chattel. In law, though not in fact, he had no family. If he was killed a few pence compensation was given to his kin, but the bulk of the money extorted from the killer was payable to the slave's master. Where a landlord had slaves, certain of them—particularly the women—would be employed in domestic duties in his house, but others might provide additional agricultural labour. They might, and often did, man the lord's ploughs and they would act as slave cowherds, swineherds, and other agricultural auxiliaries. Such slaves were allowed rations, which are described in the *Rectitudines*. 'Every slave ought to have as provisions 12 pounds of good corn and two carcases of sheep and one good cow for food and the right of cutting wood according to the custom of the estate.' He was also given extra food at Christmas and Easter and a strip of land for ploughing, or, if he was a herdsman, a young pig in a sty. It is clear that he had his own dwelling. Women slaves were expected to live on very much less and almost no meat. Those slaves who were working in the fields would be mixing there with the poorer free villagers and doing the same work. Probably as regards food and living accommodation their standard of living would be almost equivalent. This was to have consequences after the Norman Conquest.

This description of the classes of workers and the type of work done on the estate implies the existence of what is known as the open-field type of husbandry. This type predominated in

11

a wide belt of country, stretching diagonally from the Yorkshire plain to the Severn Valley, and occurred in other parts of the country if physical conditions were favourable. There were various types of open-field husbandry. There was the infield and outfield system: the infield was cultivated year after year and got all the manure available, while the outfield was normally rough pasture but every few years was broken up by what must

Open fields: Braunton Great Field, Devonshire. There are now only 12 proprietors; within living memory there were 85

have been a heavy plough (possibly drawn by more than eight oxen) and was used for a season as arable. The best-known type of open-field agriculture was that of the two- or three-field system, of which the essence was that a part of the arable was left fallow for a year to recover its fertility. There are no references to a three-field system before the Conquest, but it almost certainly existed in fertile districts, particularly if the land belonged to a church with the initiative and drive to alter tradi-

12

tional arrangements in the interests of greater productivity. In the three-field system there was an autumn sowing of rye, or wheat and rye, in one field, a spring sowing of barley or oats and beans in the second and the third was thrown open for pasture. This last would take the autumn rye or wheat sowing in the next year and so on according to a strict rotation. Within each field the villagers had their plots, in the form of long narrow strips, a furlong or furrow long and as wide as a double furrow, i.e. 'there and back' of an eight-ox plough team. There were blocks of these strips, known as shots, and a villager might have a number of strips scattered over a number of shots, giving as fair a distribution as possible of good, bad and indifferent soil. If there was one or more landlords in the village, in addition to a certain amount of enclosed land near the house, he or they would have strips in the open fields, but more than the villagers and sometimes the holdings would be concentrated. Each villager with strips bordering the outside of the field had to keep his share fenced from ploughing to harvest or he was responsible for the damage caused by straying beasts. There must have been approach ways between shots for the ploughs to reach the strips and these are answerable for some of the meandering English country lanes.

Every well-sited village would have low-lying land near a stream and the beasts of the village would pasture on this meadow after the hay had been cut, on the fallow field and on the stubble of the cornfield after the harvest, in proportion as their owners had plough land in the open fields. Each holder of strips had his own section of the meadow for the hay harvest. Probably on the outskirts of the village itself, between it and the arable land, there would be one or more *hams*, pastures reserved for certain people and limited in the number of animals allowed, so that there was better pasture for the few. Some of these privileged people seem to have been the highly necessary village craftsmen, who would not qualify for the open pasture because they had little or no arable land. Names which occur in modern villages and are suggestive of past usage are Brandersham (stock brander), Smithsham, Wontnorsham (mole catcher) and Barber's Furlong. There are also to be found in various places Parson's Close and Parson's Acre, which may

Killing the pig

have the same significance. The wasteland provided a certain amount of poor pasture and also fern and heather for bedding, litter for animals and thatching, furze and turf for fuel, small wood for hurdles and tree toppings as winter browse for livestock. The woodland, if any, was valuable not only for its timber, but as providing acorns or beechnuts which were the staple diet of the medieval pig, just as the medieval pig was the staple diet of medieval man. The pig provided meat, which lent itself easily to salting or smoking for the winter months, and also leather to be made into footwear, belts and wallets for people and into harness for animals.

Whether or not a village was dependent on one or more lords, the routine must have been the same. The village was the agricultural unit and the year's work would largely be settled in a meeting of villagers. When there was more than one lord with land and tenants in a village each lord would have his home farm or demesne and his tenants in the communal fields. In pre-Conquest England by no means every village had a lord. For

Swineherd

instance, in the more Danish regions of the country men were in the main better off and were far less often subject to a landlord. Villages would be run by the villagers for themselves, without any demesne or labour services. In such a village, the parish church would probably have been built by a group of villagers and they would also own the mill.

'And we have ordained that no man buy any property out of port over XX pence.' This is taken from a law of approximately A.D. 930, a century before our period opens. It must be explained that 'port' did not necessarily mean a seaport. It could be applied to any market town where there would be witnesses to a sale, for documentary evidence of such transactions did not exist. And let no one imagine that 20 pence was a trivial sum! Thirty pence, for instance, would buy an ox, a basic requirement in an agricultural economy. A town was a place where buying and selling naturally took place. There were towns of various kinds and of various origins in England in 1066. There were places which had been towns during the Roman occupation, which had been left derelict by the Germanic invaders of the fifth and sixth centuries, but which, because the Romans had had an eye for strategic positions and had also connected their towns by an admirable road system, came into their own again when the settlement was complete and trading centres were once more in demand. In the ninth and tenth centuries, during the Danish invasions, some of these towns attempted to refortify themselves either by repairing the old Roman walls or by ditch and palisade. Foremost among these towns was London, which, because of its geographical position, is and was and always has been the natural commercial capital of the country.

Smaller towns grew up naturally at the intersections of important roads, at places where rivers could be forded or bridged and on sea coasts with inland communications.

Another type of town was a deliberate creation and was fortified from the beginning. Alfred, in his wars against the Danes, began the policy of building *burhs*—fortified enclosures—at certain strategic points. Such a burh or borough might be a vill fortified. It would then attract a higher population by its offer of personal freedom and comparative security from attack.

The High Seat: after-dinner drinking

Sites in the borough were offered on payment of a small annual rent to the king. This differed from place to place but averaged about one shilling. The holder of a burgage tenement had the right to dispose of it at will. Neighbouring thegns would not only have a town house for their own occupation but might also take up a number of sites for their men. The thegn's town house would probably be a replica of his country one, an all-purpose hall where he and his family dined and the rest of the household lived, and a bower or chamber where he and his family slept. The hall furnishings would be elementary, a seat or 'settle' for the lord and his companions and removable trestle tables with benches. The Anglo-Saxons were notorious eaters and drinkers. After the main meal was over the tables would be removed and the rest of the day spent in drinking and listening to minstrels singing or reciting in Anglo-Saxon. The ladies would retire to the bower, furnished with bench beds along the walls.

Curtained beds

Banquet—a toast

These were used as seats during the day and fitted with straw mattresses when required. The bed coverings and the curtains, which secured a modicum of privacy, were the only evidence of luxury.

The thegns and the better-off townsfolk would buy up the surplus dairy produce of the surrounding villages and they would be the best and most appreciative customers of the bold trader who, in the words of Aelfric in the early eleventh century, sailed over the seas with his wares and returned with 'purple and silk, precious gems and gold, rare garments and spices, wine and oil, ivory and brass, copper and tin, sulphur, glass and such things', which he hoped to sell at a profit to maintain himself and his wife and children. An exaggerated inventory of an eleventh-century pedlar's pack no doubt, but there must have been trade in many of the items for Aelfric to be aware of it. For fishermen who lived within easy reach of a town there was a ready market for their wares. Says Aelfric's fisherman: 'I cannot

17

catch as much as I could sell'. Fish was an important item in the diet of the medieval Christian and it was not readily available in all parts of the country. Salt was in demand for fish as for meat, and being a localised product it was an important trading commodity. Iron was another important natural resource which was localised. William of Poitiers, writing not long after the Conquest, tells us that the Anglo-Saxons had a great reputation for metal work, and it is permissible to assume that a town like Gloucester, whose proximity to the bloomeries of the Forest of Dean made it an iron centre, owed its prosperity to the sale of iron products. Edward the Confessor relied on Gloucester for the nails for his ships.

Trade on anything other than a purely local basis requires money and the amount needed varies with the volume of trade. It was therefore a matter of convenience for the king to license moneyers and mints in a great many towns. There were probably about 70 mints up and down the country in 1066, according to estimates made from coins recovered. There was a single centre, London, where the dies were cut, and from these each moneyer had to work. Each time the die was changed, approximately at three-year intervals before Henry II, he had to pay a fee to the king. The coins varied somewhat, but in the main they carried on one side the image and superscription of the king and on the other a cross inscribed in a circle and the name of the moneyer and the mint. In so far as our information is complete, we can tell roughly from the number of moneyers in a town its relative wealth and importance. Very small towns would have one, somewhat larger ones three, York had ten and London

Twelfth-century iron pits at Bentley Grange, Yorkshire. The bushes mark the position of the shallow shafts and the mounds are spoil heaps, about six feet high

18

Silver penny of Henry II, minted by Hugo of York

headed the list with 20. The temptation to produce bad money must have been great, but the punishment was fitted to the crime and the moneyer's name on the coin made concealment difficult. The pre-Conquest penalty was loss of a hand, which was then nailed to the smithy door. No change seems to have been made by the Normans. In 1125 we are told that the Chief Justiciar, Bishop Roger of Salisbury, on the order of Henry I, summoned all the moneyers to Winchester and, because they had 'foredone all the land with their great quantity of false money', they were all mutilated according to the law, 94 of them, leaving only three whole men, three Winchester moneyers. The silver penny was the standard coin of England. There was no gold coinage at this period and, with the possible exception of a halfpenny under Henry I, there was no lesser denomination. If less was wanted, the cross on the reverse of the coin could be used as a guide for cutting it into what were literally halfpennies and farthings.

We have no means of knowing exactly how many inhabitants there were in English boroughs in 1066. Domesday Book is our best guide and that gives the number of households, which clearly includes all the members of each family and probably servants also. Thus any estimate of the number of people depends on an inspired guess as to the average number per household. For London and Winchester, the commercial and political capitals, we have no Domesday entries and therefore no figures for the eleventh century. The evidence of the coinage as to the wealth and importance of London in 1066 is borne out by Duke William's attitude to it, his attempt to woo the Londoners by a grant of their ancient privileges and his healthy respect for its citizens' capacity for rude force, as shown by his refusal to enter the city until suitable fortifications had been prepared for him.

The thegns or gentry, originally an aristocracy of service, had largely become an aristocracy by birth, inheriting their huge blood price of 1,200 silver shillings, but the class was not entirely rigid. It could be recruited from men who had acquired land, at least five hides (or 600 acres), together with the responsibilities of landownership—such as maintenance of a church, and the obligation to follow the king to war. Such men were promoted to the 1,200-shilling *wergild* and, if the family maintained the position for three generations, the rank and the *wergild* became hereditary. The class could also be recruited from merchants who had 'thrived three times over the sea at their own expense'. It was from this class of men and from members of the royal house and from the bishops that the governing class of the country was drawn. Under the king, the most important men were the earls, who represented the king's political power in the provinces. In the time of Edward the Confessor the most outstanding were Wessex, under the house of Godwin, Mercia under Leofric and Northumbria until 1055 under Siward (the man who defeated Macbeth of Scotland). The average number of earls in England under Edward was six or seven, of whom one was a Norman cousin of the king, established on the Welsh border in what is now Herefordshire. These earls, particularly the three greater ones, were very influential in the councils of the king (*see* p. 125) as were also the bishops, but the routine of government was carried out through an official

A thegn

who still bears his Anglo-Saxon name, *scir-gerefa*, shire reeve or sheriff, although his functions and powers have both changed and declined over the centuries. He acted as the king's representative in the shire, carried out the king's orders, led the shire militia and presided over the shire court, jointly with the local bishop. Twice a year all the freemen of the shire were expected to be present at this court, which was a combined county council and a court of law. In addition there

20

were two other meetings in Anglo-Saxon England to which the freeman owed attendance and which had considerable importance in his life, for the countryman the hundred moot (in Danish England the wapentake) and for the burgess the borough court. The hundred and the wapentake were sub-divisions of a shire. The borough court met three times a year but beyond that we know nothing about it before 1066. The hundred court consisted nominally of all freemen resident within the hundred boundaries. It met every four weeks, normally in the open air, and the location of the moot is preserved by many place-names. It was generally presided over by the reeve, a royal officer, although the king could and did grant the right to hold the hundred court and collect its fines to certain of his nobles or to the great abbeys of England. The Abbey of St Edmund held eight-and-a-half hundreds—a small shire! In such a case the steward of the owner would preside.

What sort of army had the English? Every freeman was expected to fight when called upon, but, as he was not trained to fight and as his weapons were a scratch lot and as his pace was that of a foot-slogger, it is difficult to see him as of much military value. In fact King Alfred had found that it was of little use to defeat the Danes unless he could follow up his victory, and the Danes were always horsed. So, although the obligation to fight remained universal, in fact the real burden of service lay on the landed thegns and the churls (ceorls—freemen of the 200-shilling class) who qualified for the thegn class. Some burgesses got rid of their commitment by combining, as a borough, to pay for a certain number of properly equipped men to follow the king. Cnut added another element, his huscarls or bodyguard. These were paid soldiers, but it soon became customary to settle them on the land. The huscarls and the thegns formed the back-bone of the army which followed King Harold to Stamford Bridge in Yorkshire in 1066, to fight and defeat the hitherto victorious invading army of Harold Hardrada, the King of Norway. It was these same huscarls and thegns, fewer in number and very weary, who hastened south after the battle to meet the new threat from William, Duke of Normandy, and who formed the hard core of the gallant army of resistance on Senlac Hill—

Saxons (on foot) and Normans in battle

augmented by lesser thegns and freemen armed with the tools of husbandry—to fight and lose what has been called the last battle of the Stone Age, Hastings, 1066. The English and Danish thegns, who made up the armies of the pre-Conquest period, did not fight on horseback. The Normans did. On the Continent fighting on horseback had been possible and customary ever since the introduction of the stirrup from the East had provided the horseman with the stability necessary to couch his lance and use his shield. It has been said that the true horse soldier must be made in extreme youth. However that may be, Englishmen had not learned the art. We are told in the Anglo-Saxon Chronicle under the year 1055, that, when Griffith of Wales led an army over the border, Earl Ralph, King Edward's cousin, gathered a large force at Hereford town 'but before any spear had been thrown, the English army fled because they were on horseback'.

There is one section of the community which has so far been omitted, yet it played a very large part in the life of the period—the Church. The English Church was rather out of step with the continental Church in the years before 1066. The bishoprics were few and were sometimes centred in places which were no longer populous or important. York had only one suffragan bishopric—Durham. In the southern province the small village of Dorchester on Thames provided the title for a see which covered most of the land between the Humber and the Thames.

To the west of it were Worcester and Lichfield, to the east Elmham, another village. In the south the bishoprics were rather thicker on the ground, but again Selsey and Sherborne were villages. Most of the later English parishes were in being, but there were still a few 'minsters' left over from an earlier age, served by groups of clergy whose function it was to fulfil the spiritual needs of a considerable area. Something of a return to this group ministry is advocated now as a means of dealing with the shortcomings of the parish system, particularly in towns. Most of the parish priests, nominated by the owner of the church, were drawn from the free peasant class, literate only in a very rudimentary way, sharing the agricultural life of their flock and generally endowed with about twice the standard number of strips in the open fields. There were monasteries, which had a very important influence as almost the only educational institutions, but, although there had been many new foundations in the tenth century, there were only 35 monasteries and six nunneries in 1066. Many of the churches of Anglo-Saxon England have disappeared, built as they were, like their domestic counterparts, of ephemeral materials, but in ecclesiastical architecture the scene is not quite so blank as in domestic. Some churches were built of stone and not all of them were pulled down to make way for the more magnificent structures of a later age. The whole or parts of some 300 of these churches have survived and from the south of England to Northumberland it is possible for the searching eye to find one of these relics and to reconstruct an Anglo-Saxon church. In general they were very small. Probably they were adequate for the population they served, even though the proportion of it which was churchgoing was much nearer 100 per cent than

Escomb, Co. Durham: a typical Saxon church

23

it is today. But smallness was forced on the Anglo-Saxon by the absence of building technique. The walls were solid enough to stand up unaided and the window apertures were small and in no way weakened the fabric. The problem was to roof a space whether by timber or by stone.

This then was the England whose wealth and comparative stability tempted two adventurers in 1066, when the new English king, Harold Godwinson, was a promoted earl with no dynastic claims on the loyalty of his fellow earls. The first adventurer to land on English soil, the Norwegian Harold Hardrada, ultimately got the seven feet of English earth which Harold of England promised him 'because he was taller than most'. The other adventurer, Duke William of Normandy, lucky in that he was able to land while Harold was busy against his namesake in the north, won the Battle of Hastings and with surprising ease got himself accepted as King of England.

Further Reading

D. Whitelock, *The Beginnings of English Society*
F. M. Stenton, *Anglo-Saxon England* (to 1087)
D. C. Douglas, *English Historical Documents, Vol. II: 1042–1189*
C. N. L. Brooke, *A History of England, Vol. II. From Alfred to Henry III, 871–1272*

II

An Alien King
and Aristocracy

William was king of England and his army of adventurers were soon to spread like locusts over the land, their Anglo-Saxon predecessors being dead or deprived of their property—and either sunk into the mass of the peasantry or gone into exile. At this time the bodyguard of the Emperor at Constantinople begins to wear a distinctly Anglo-Saxon complexion! From the point of view of native English literature and art the change was catastrophic. Those now in a position to give patronage to literature and the arts neither understood the language nor had any feeling for the finer products of English craftsmanship. What manner of men were these, who now formed the governing class of a divided society, the two parts of which did not speak or understand each other's tongue?

In 1066 and during the years following the Conquest, the life of the king was governed by certain factors. He and his followers were hated foreigners on English soil and had so to order their lives that defence and self-protection were paramount. This stage lasted for the greater part of William's reign. There were other factors of a more permanent nature. Many of these combined to ensure that the king, with his court, passed much of his life in transit from one place to another. In the first place, the king, who kept one quarter of England for his own use, had estates in various parts of the country. All estates (manors) were geared to supply the lord's household with the basic necessities of life. If the lord had more than one manor there arose the problem of using their produce. The most usual solution was for him to pass his time between them and to consume the produce of each on the spot, or at least to use on one manor the tribute of nearby manors. The same applied in great measure to the king, although he would usually have some other purpose than the bread and cheese one to direct his journeys. The Norman king was both Head of State, Prime Minister and Cabinet, and Commander-in-Chief, and he held these offices in his own person, not by deputy, except on occasions when he was out of the country, that is in Normandy. In the interests of making his government felt, as well as of putting down revolts, William travelled over most of England. He had no definite capital, although London was politically and commercially the most important town in England. On his travels he made use of the royal castles, which provided cover and protection if little in the way of comfort.

Although in the early years of the Conquest the interests of the new Norman baronage largely coincided with those of the monarchy, since they were both concerned with establishing and maintaining the new régime and defending their land rights against the dispossessed English landowners, yet William could not wholly trust his barons. This was one of his reasons for carrying on Edward the Confessor's custom of holding great meetings in three important towns in the south, Gloucester at Christmas, Winchester at Easter and London at Whitsun. At these meetings William wore his crown and kept great state. All his more important subjects were expected to attend. He was able to impress with his majesty and to watch for possible conspiracies. The custom was carried on by William II but dropped by Henry I. These meetings made three fixed dates in the king's year whenever he was in England, and they demanded three outsize halls in which such large assemblies could for-gather.

Busy as his life undoubtedly was, the king had to have some recreation and for the Norman kings there was no choice. William I 'loved the stags as if he were their father'. There were many natural forests in England. In fact, as we shall see, one of the main tasks of the next century in England would be to reclaim much woodland and turn it into good agricultural land; but there were not enough forests or they were not suitably sited for William. He cleared agricultural land and destroyed some houses to create the New Forest in Hampshire and he extended other existing forests. This policy of afforestation was followed by subsequent kings to the great detriment of many of their subjects, for the laws which governed the

Hawking

king's forests and protected his sport were strict and harsh and they were enforced by special officers and courts. Whenever possible the Norman and Angevin kings repaired to their forests to hunt and, for the provision of shelter and the apparatus of living for themselves and their followers, hunting lodges were required.

So the kings from 1066 to 1216 required two types of accommodation, castles and hunting lodges, and the first two kings required in addition commodious halls at Gloucester, Winchester and London.

For the three outsize gatherings needing three outsize halls William I was following in the steps of his predecessor and he seems to have inherited buildings which served for a time after the Conquest. A royal palace at Gloucester is mentioned in a contemporary life of Edward. It was probably the old palace of Kingsholm north of the city and referred to as the king's hall in documents of the twelfth and thirteenth centuries. King Stephen used it rather than the castle in his triumphal entry into Gloucester in 1138, and Henry III was escorted from 'the kingshome at Gloucestere' to his coronation in the Abbey Church in 1216. Thereafter it is lost to history. In Winchester there was a royal palace, but it was left to Edward's widow, Queen Edith, and William had to build another. He gave the monks of the New Minster a manor and a church in exchange for land in the

27

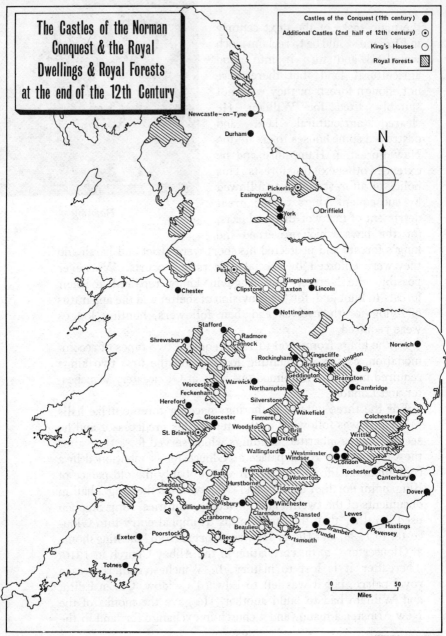

The Castles of the Norman Conquest & the Royal Dwellings & Royal Forests at the end of the 12th Century

Castles of the Conquest (11th century) ●
Additional Castles (2nd half of 12th century) ◉
King's Houses ○
Royal Forests

N

Newcastle-on-Tyne
Durham
Pickering
Easingwold
York
Driffield
Peak
Kingshaugh
Chester
Clipstone
Laxton
Lincoln
Nottingham
Stafford
Shrewsbury
Radmore
Cannock
Rockingham
Kingscliffe
Norwich
Kinver
Brigstock
Huntingdon
Geddington
Ely
Worcester
Warwick
Brampton
Feckenham
Northampton
Cambridge
Hereford
Silverstone
Gloucester
Finmere
Wakefield
St. Briavels
Woodstock
Colchester
Brill
Writtle
Oxford
Havering
Wallingford
Westminster
Windsor
London
Rochester
Bath
Freemantle
Wolverton
Canterbury
Cheddar
Hurstborne
Tidgrove
Dover
Salisbury
Winchester
Gillingham
Cranborne
Clarendon
Stansted
Lewes
Beaulieu
Hastings
Exeter
Poorstock
Bere
Bramber
Pevensey
Portsmouth
Arundel
Totnes

0   50
Miles

ARTHUR BANKS MAPS LTD.

The Confessor's Palace at Westminster

city, 'upon which in the fourth year of his reign he built a new
hall and palace in handsome fashion'. It was subsequently
recorded that 12 burgesses living in the High Street had been
evicted to make way for the king's house and that a neighbouring street had been obstructed by the king's kitchen. William I's
house was burnt down in 1140 and was never rebuilt. The obvious inference is that it was of wood. It is also likely that, as in so
many medieval houses, the kitchen was a separate building. For
London (or Westminster) we have pictorial evidence, for the
Bayeux Tapestry shows us a stylised version of the Confessor's
palace. Whether it sufficed for William I it is difficult to say.
His healthy respect for 'the fierce and vast' populace of London
makes it possible that he himself stayed in his wooden castle, the
predecessor of the White Tower. He may even have stayed in a
castle at Winchester, for one was built there at about the same
time as his new palace. We learn from the Peterborough Chronicle that William II, in 1097, began the building of a great hall
at Westminster, portions of which remain to this day in spite of
extensive modification and rebuilding in the fourteenth century.
This must have been one of the earliest non-military and non-
ecclesiastical buildings to have been constructed in stone. It was
an enormous hall, 240 by $67\frac{1}{2}$ feet, possibly the largest of its
kind in Europe at that time. It seems to have had four doors,

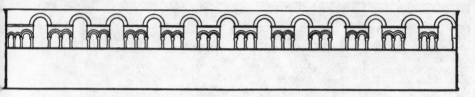

two in the end walls and one in each side near the north end of the hall. These may have been cut off from the main body of the hall by a wooden partition screen. There are certain irregularities in the arcading and buttresses of the two sides, a discrepancy of about four feet, which suggest either that so large a building was beyond the planning capacity of the royal masons in 1097, or, more likely, that it was built round a smaller wooden hall, which was still in use during the building, thereby making it more difficult to take accurate measurements. This smaller hall might have been that in use before and after 1066. The present hall, incorporating the lower part of the walls of William's hall, dates from the fourteenth century, and is still an integral part of the palace of Westminster. It is used on such solemn occasions as the lying in state of kings and statesmen.

Castles form a much bigger topic. They are definitely a Norman importation, though a few were erected before 1066 by Norman followers of King Edward. The Anglo-Saxons and the Danes in England knew only the ditched and walled or palisaded burh. In fact burh means a hedge or palisade and even the royal palaces of pre-Conquest days had no more defensive apparatus

Raising the motte at Hastings

than this. To William the castle was an essential part of his strategy for keeping England in subjection once he had conquered it. He may possibly have brought his first castle with him in prefabricated parts. In the Bayeux Tapestry we can see his men digging for the mound

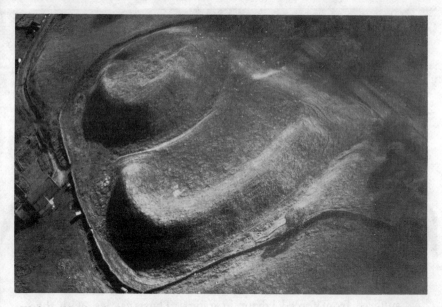

Elsdon, Northumberland: a small baronial 'motte-and-bailey castle of the twelfth century. Note the ditch round the kidney-shaped bailey and the motte, and also the ditch separating the motte from the more expendable bailey

or motte at Hastings and assembling the superstructure on it. We also know from a contemporary writer, William of Poitiers, that when William accepted the crown of England and moved to London for his coronation 'he sent forward to London picked men to build a fortress in the city and to make suitable preparations for the coming of royal splendour'. This took a few days, during which time William waited on the outskirts of London. The fortress, clearly a timber structure, was erected on the site of the future White Tower and a section of the old Roman wall of London provided protection for the bailey or courtyard. All William's early castles, and those of his barons, must have been of this primitive type. The best site in a town would be chosen, without regard for existing buildings on the land. In Lincoln 166 houses were demolished to make way for the castle, in Cambridge 27 and in York and many other towns varying numbers. The greatest work was the digging of the ditch and the throwing up of the great mound, sometimes 100 feet in diameter. When this had to be done in the space of days, several in London, eight at Dover in 1066 and eight for a second castle at York in 1069, it is clear that many poor men must have

Defending the castle at Dinan

suffered from forced labour in gangs. These castles, with the large mound surrounded by ditch and stockade and surmounted by a wooden tower, often on stilts to allow for free movement of the garrison, the whole completed by a large bailey also protected by a stockade and often by a ditch, could withstand the type of attack that could be mounted in the eleventh century, except for the danger of fire.

However, the Normans brought with them not only carpenters but masons, and both the king and his greater barons proceeded to replace certain of their castles with more solid structures of stone. The first to be so treated was the king's fortress in London, where the work was under the overall supervision of Gundulf, Bishop of Rochester, who was known to be very competent at building in stone. Colchester was designed on a similar but somewhat larger scale. Colchester is a ruin, but the White Tower remains, with certain modifications, to show us what conditions of life could be for a wealthy king in the eleventh century. The walls are 15 feet thick at the base, diminishing to 12 feet at the top. The main structure is of rubble with very open joints, characteristic of early Norman work, while the plinth, quoins and pilasters are believed to be of Kentish rag, the only building stone within easy reach of London. It was three storeys high, with the entrance at first floor level through a fore-

The White Tower, the keep of the Tower of London, 1078–90 (note the wide-jointed masonry)

building, which has since disappeared. The king's dwelling was on the main floor, with great hall, chamber and chapel and certain private apartments in a mural gallery. The ground floor, with no windows and no access from outside, contained stores of food and arms and the dungeons.

The White Tower and Colchester keep were really fortified palaces rather than just fortresses, and if they suggest little comfort by twentieth-century standards they must have offered well above the average of the eleventh century, at least for the lord and his family, who would be the only ones considered. For the majority of the royal household the great hall would be an all-purpose room. Trestle tables were erected for mealtimes and removed to provide sleeping room at night. The benches might remain as beds for the lucky ones. Rushes provided the removeable floor covering and these were usually changed when the king was expected. The Norman kings kept most of their treasure at Winchester, as had their predecessors, but the necessary funds for day-to-day use, as also the king's jewels and his robes, would be kept in his bedroom, or in a small adjoining chamber which came to be known as the wardrobe. Although most of the wooden castles built by William I and his barons were strengthened or rebuilt in stone during the late eleventh and the twelfth centuries, the process was slow and wooden castles were still being erected even at the end of the twelfth century. They were cheaper, easier to build and sometimes more convenient. In 1171 Henry II sent prefabricated timber castles to Ireland and Richard I took them to Sicily and the East when he went on the Third Crusade. The wooden tower at York was replaced by another tower, also of wood, after 1190, and the present stone keep was not built

Castle Hedingham, Essex: the great hall, measuring 39' × 31' × 26' (note mural galleries)

34

until the mid-thirteenth century. King John made provision for the repair of his wooden castles in Shropshire in 1204. They evidently still had their uses. However, most of the wooden structures had been rebuilt in stone before the end of the twelfth century, in the generality of cases on the same pattern as the old motte and bailey, but with a stone keep. This was rarely built on the old mound at this time because it took centuries for an artificial mound to settle sufficiently to provide a firm foundation for a heavy stone keep.

Rochester Castle, Kent: the interior of the keep, showing sockets for wooden floors

For our knowledge of the castles of the period we rely to a great extent on the actual remains which exist today, but we have also, from the beginning of Henry II's reign, a set of financial records known as the Pipe Rolls, which give us valuable information about the money spent by Henry and his sons on their castles and other dwellings. Most of the castles erected by the barons during the civil wars of Stephen's reign (1135–54) were of earth and timber and it was Henry's policy to destroy them. He himself spent large, in fact fabulous, sums on certain of his castles in the second part of his reign. Newcastle-upon-Tyne had been erected by Robert, son of William I, in 1080 on a steep headland overlooking the Tyne, but it was not until 1157 that it came permanently into the possession of Henry II and not until 1168 that major work was undertaken on it. In the next ten years £1,144 was spent on a stone keep surrounded by a bailey wall. Dover was another castle, a more elaborate one, on which vast sums were spent. These two suggest defence against the Scots in the north and threats from the Continent in the south-east, rather than protection against rebels within the country. Possibly for this reason, that castles were not in constant use in actual warfare as they were on the Continent, English military architecture lagged behind the times. Across the

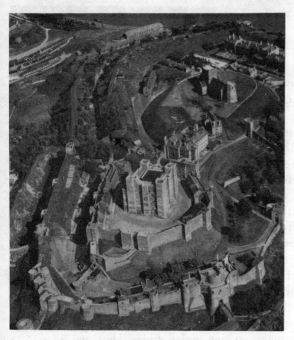

Dover Castle, Kent (late Henry II) showing inner and outer bailey and the possibility of domestic buildings within the bailey

Channel, first the polygonal and then the circular keep had been adopted as providing fewer blind spots in the defence. Both these types were tried out in England, but they did not supplant the rectangular keep.

The building of a stone wall round the bailey, which was often what was intended in the Pipe Rolls by the term 'castle', meant that the bailey provided better protection, and that the living quarters, which had either been included in the keep, crowded together as separate units on top of the mound or placed precariously in an ill-defended bailey, could now be built in wood or stone—and it was usually wood even in the thirteenth century —as a permanent feature of the bailey. Many of the expenses which occur in the Pipe Rolls of the late twelfth century are for the king's houses in his castles. This was a very important development, as it allowed for private quarters for the great men of the household as well as for the king and queen. These baileys sometimes covered several acres and there are references to gardens. There must have been great changes in living conditions, even in castles. Castle guard, with a proper quota of knights, was part of the service which a tenant in chief contracted to perform for a certain period each year. The spell of duty of each lord would come round regularly and in many cases these landowners built their own houses in the bailey, ready for occupation at the appropriate time. The need for defence was never entirely absent during these centuries, but, except in periods of civil war, it became less necessary for the king to live within fortifications. Not only was more care spent on the embellishment of the royal quarters within castles, but also the king and his family spent less of their time in such buildings. When William II built his new hall at Westminster it was on the site of Edward the Confessor's palace, cheek by jowl with the Confessor's new Abbey. William intended to erect more buildings on the site, but he died in 1100, and the terms 'old palace' and 'new palace', which were applied to the royal halls at Westminster, suggest that parts of Edward's palace were still being used. There was a small hall for everyday use, mentioned for the first time in 1167, and a great chamber projecting from it at right angles. This was one large room under Henry III, but it may have been divided previously into a king's and a queen's chamber. There were two chapels in the twelfth century, the famous St Stephen's Chapel and St John's Chapel. This was the principal palace of the king and it was here that buildings grew up to accommodate what later became

government offices, particularly the Exchequer with its tower, from a room at the top of which the Treasurer, Richard Fitz Nigel, used to watch the traffic on the Thames.

Orford Castle, Suffolk: the polygonal keep, 1165–73

The three great palaces and the numerous castles planted all over the country may seem ample provision, even for the peripatetic kings of the eleventh and twelfth centuries, but these were not all. The preferred places of stay were in or on the edge of the royal forests. Many, if not most, of the hunting lodges must have been of timber. One such was at Kinver in Staffordshire. There was probably a house there in William II's

37

reign but in the years 1184–88 work was carried out on the orders of Henry II, making a ditch round the king's house and improving the king's chamber at a cost of over £22. Then the absentee king, Richard I, decided to rebuild, on not quite the same site. The new lodge consisted of a hall with its offices, a kitchen, a chamber, a gaol, a gateway with a brattice and an encircling palisade 16 feet high to keep out intruders. A fishpond was formed by damming the River Stour. As the total bill, including equipment, was £24 18s. 9d. it is obvious that timber was the material used. King John stayed at Kinver on more than one occasion. With the limited accommodation no one, other than the king himself with his chamber, could expect any privacy or comfort. Kinver, and there were many others like it, remained just a hunting lodge, but there were others which began life humbly but, owing to their attraction for various kings, became in effect palaces. Two such were Clarendon and Woodstock, both favourite haunts of Henry II. These were ultimately built mainly in stone and were able to accommodate large councils. In fact they became so big that they sprouted dependencies, like the two Trianons at Versailles. Woodstock had its Everswell, which in the time of Henry III became a place of retreat for the royal family, with gardens and pleasaunces. In the reign of Henry II it had another function, for it was here that Henry kept his favourite mistress, the fair Rosamund Clifford, and her chamber still bore the name of Rosamund's Bower a century later. A list of the king's various houses would be a long one, making the Buckingham Palace, Windsor, Sandringham and Balmoral of our own monarchy seem very modest.

These houses were all used, although different kings had different favourites. It has already been said that most of the kings spent a good proportion of their time abroad. We know, for instance, that Henry II spent only a third of his 35 years' reign here and Richard I only six months of a ten years' reign. If the English periods had to cover sojourns at most of the castles and other houses, it follows that a good deal of time must have been spent on the roads and that each of the king's journeys would be a major operation. The Pipe Rolls are our guides as to the expenses allowed the sheriffs for transporting various items, including the vast quantities of wine consumed by the royal household. Much of the king's treasure had to be carried and so had chests containing official documents. Not only the king and his vast household, but the great prelates and barons, who met him in council far from their base, must

The king taking counsel with his barons

have cluttered up the dusty or muddy tracks, which passed for roads in twelfth-century England. Walter Map, in his *Courtiers' Trifles*, described Henry II as being 'tolerant of the discomforts of dust and mud'. One gets the impression that Walter wearied of the constant journeyings. He looked back nostalgically to the good old days of Henry I, which, seen in retrospect, seemed so much better ordered than those of his grandson. Journeys there had to be, but Henry I's were planned in advance.

> He arranged with great precision, and publicly gave notice of, the days of his travelling and of his stay, with the number of days and the names of the vills, so that everyone might know without chance of a mistake the course of his living month by month. Nothing was done without preparation or without previous arrangement or in a hurry. Everything was managed as befitted a king and with proper control. Hence there was eager sailing from beyond the seas to his court, of merchants with wares and luxuries for sale, and likewise from all parts of England, so that nowhere save about the king, wherever he went, were there plentiful markets.

Of his own master, Henry II, Walter Map wrote: 'He was always on the move, travelling in unbearably long stages like a post, and in this respect merciless beyond measure to the household that accompanied him.' John seems to have resembled his father in his liking for rapid movement. He covered sometimes 40 or 50 miles a day—strenuous going in the days of horse travel. On his final journey, when he lost part of his baggage in the Wash, he

seems to have arranged for some to go to Grimsby by water.
He himself, with his cavalcade and about 12 waggons and the
pack horses, would go by the causeway across the tidal area of
the Wash. He was so impatient that he could not wait for the
tide, so the slow-moving baggage train was swept away. We
do not know the extent of the loss as John died soon afterwards. He may have been robbed at his death by members of his

Wine transport. For long distances horses would be used

household, who could cover up their crime by exaggerating the
losses on the fateful journey. Work is being carried out now
with a view to locating the exact course of the thirteenth-
century causeway. Presumably efforts will be made to recover
the treasure.

In the days when the essence of government was the king, the
king's household and his court were largely identical. His high-
ranking officials bore titles suggesting domestic duties. The
fact is that, when the king was all-powerful, it was those in daily
contact with him who had the most influence, and the court must
frequently have been a place for intrigue and jockeying for
position. At any rate, so it appeared to Walter Map, who spent
most of his life in it. He said that the Court was not hell but was

as like it as a horse's shoe is like a mare's. The chamberlains who looked after the king's bedchamber were at the centre of power. Much of the king's treasure was actually kept in his chamber. The particular chamberlain whose job it was to take charge of it became the Treasurer, quite soon after the Conquest. The Master Chamberlain, with the overall supervision of the Chamber, was one of the highest officials at court. The Chancellor, originally the chaplain who sat behind a screen (*cancella*), did the king's writing and took charge of his seal, was not a very highly placed official, but as writing and sealing became more important aspects of government so did the Chancellor become head of the writing office and ultimately one of the most important men in the country. His career began with the Norman Conquest and by the end of the eleventh century he could generally aspire to a bishopric, but he would regard this as promotion and resign his Chancellorship. Thomas Becket, Henry II's Chancellor, became Archbishop of Canterbury and refused to retain his previous office, even at the King's request. Yet at the end of the century Hubert Walter was both Chancellor and Archbishop, and as such was John's principal minister until he died in 1205.

Fortunately we know something of the household of the king at the end of Henry I's reign and at the beginning of the thirteenth century. We have a document, the *Constitutio Domus Regis* (Constitution of the King's Household), which probably represents an attempt by Henry I to cure the disorders of his own and his brother's reigns. As more records began to be kept early in the next century we have even fuller information for the reign of John. In 1135 the heads of the chief departments received the generous—and it was generous—sum of five shillings a day. They would, if on duty, feed at the royal table, but for extra food and for light they were allowed certain rations, which differed for the various offices. The Chancellor was the best off, as he got his full 5s. whether or not he was resident, and also what would seem to us extravagant supplementary rations of best and ordinary bread, four gallons of dessert wine and the same of ordinary wine, one large wax candle and forty candle ends. Some of the other heads of departments, such

41

as the Head Steward, the Master Butler, the Master Chamberlain
and the Treasurer, had 5s. a day if they ate out but only 3s. 6d.
if they fed at the king's table, and their supplementary rations
lacked the luxury element of the superior simnel bread and the
dessert wine. These exalted officials were all in receipt of landed
estates in return for their services, and the services were, in most
cases, more honorary than actual, although they had responsibility for the work of their departments and were in attendance
on the king and at his disposal for advice and counsel. On cere-
monial occasions it was their duty and privilege to perform their
offices in person and to receive as their rewards the silver cups,
bowls or other utensils used by the king and his guests. We
have many contemporary accounts of unseemly squabbles in
the king's presence, and sometimes even the use of physical
violence, in the assertion of the right to perform menial tasks
for the king at great ceremonies. Something of all this, without
the unseemly behaviour, remains to this day in the offices of
the Earl Marshal and the Lord Chamberlain.

In the day-to-day business of life the menial tasks were performed by menials, who were paid as such:

> the bearer of the king's bed shall eat in the house and have 1½d. a
> day for his man and one pack horse. The ewer [waterman] has
> double diet and when the king goes on a journey 1d. for drying the
> king's clothes [evidence of the weather hazards of twelfth-century
> travel] and when the king bathes 4d. except on the three great
> feasts of the year. The wages of the washerwoman are in doubt.

This doubt was to some extent resolved by the end of our period
when the Household Accounts show us that periodically
Florence, the washerwoman, received 1s. 6d. for shoes. The
same accounts portray King John as a model of cleanliness. In
addition to his two free baths in the six months from January,
1209, John had eight baths for which he paid his ewer a fee. The
ewer by this time had also achieved a basic regular wage, ½d.
a day. A small department in 1135 was that of the king's
tailor, who was to eat in his own house and to have 1½d. a day
for his man. It is quite clear from the Constitutio that the king's
household was completely mobile. The king had his houses up

and down the country, but he carried
with him most of the appurtenances
of his daily life. We find listed 'two
pack horses of the chapel, each 1*d*.
a day and 1*d*. a month for shoeing
them'. There are horses for the
upper kitchen and for the great kitchen and a bearer and packhorse
for the king's bed. There is a tent
keeper, who is to eat in the house
and who has livery for one man and
one packhorse when the tents are

Tent

moved. Clearly some nights under canvas are envisaged in the
royal wanderings. There are four bakers in the pantry department, two serving indoors and two going ahead to have ready 40
superior simnels, 150 salt simnels and 260 bakers' loaves. There
are cooks and scullions and ushers of the kitchen with their men,
serjeants of the kitchen, a cook for the king's personal servants,
an usher of the roasting house and his man, a serjeant to receive
the venison, slaughterers and many others. The kitchen staff
serves under the Master Dispenser of the Larder, a permanent
official at 2*s*. a day and his food, who, with the Master Dispenser
of Bread, serves under the Steward, a 5*s*-a-day man and of baronial status. The word 'larder' is suggestive of the importance of
the pig in the commissariat! There is a whole staff connected
with the king's sport, hunting, which also contributed substan-
tially to the household's meat diet. All the trained personnel
followed the king. Some would even operate on both sides of the
Channel, but there must always have been additional, unskilled
labour, recruited on a local basis.

Life then was arduous for the Norman and Angevin kings.
They would arrive at their destination for the night, the early
kings to a primitive castle, a wooden tower on a mound with
perhaps separate wooden hall and chamber and open-air kitchen.
Later kings, except on campaigns, would look for somewhat
greater comfort, either in the numerous unfortified king's houses
or in castles, which were acquiring domestic amenities within an
encircling earthwork or wall. When the king's destination was

43

known in advance, orders would have been sent to the local
sheriff to put the king's house in order, possibly specific orders
about renovations to the royal chamber or chambers. Often the
king's engineer or carpenter would have been sent with a staff
and would requisition local labour. Fresh rushes would have
been strewn on floors, fuel would have been got in and if necessary, temporary kitchens erected. The advance bakers would have
bought the flour and baked for the party. The Bayeux Tapestry

Duke William and his brothers feasting

shows Duke William and his brothers feasting with some decorum
in conditions more difficult than those engendered by the constant
royal journeyings. The Court seems to have had two meals a day
and, if the supplementary rations allowed to members of the household are anything to go by, quite substantial snacks in addition.
Meatless meals were the rule for certain days and throughout
Lent, and to cope with this various measures were taken. Fishponds are to be found in many of the king's houses and even
castles. Two mills were destroyed to make William I a fishpond

in York. Eels from the millstream were a frequent form of rent payable by the miller. Rivers and the sea were important food suppliers and certain manors, for instance in the region of the Severn, gave much of their annual render in fish. King John seems to have been allergic to a too-frequent fish diet, for in 1209 he was pay-

Fishponds at Harrington, Northamptonshire. Small pond probably breeding pond; feeder channels on left, overflow on right. (Breech in nearside dam is modern)

ing 9s. 4½d. to 100 poor men when he ate twice on Friday, probably meat. Much of the meat in winter must have been salted and spices from the East were imported to make it more palatable or to disguise an already too-strong flavour.

The king's table, as it appears in illustrations of the Norman period, like the tables of the Anglo-Saxon kings, was covered with a cloth (laying the table) and the servitors who handed the wine cup and the dishes on bended knee also carried napkins. In the *Constitutio* the king's napier had a pack-horse and 1d. a month for shoeing him. The bread seems to have been served in the form of flat cakes, decorated with a cross or other design. The king would have wheaten bread, as would his greatest subjects and many others aspired to it. For the lower ranks rye bread was normal. There were dishes for fish, and meat was often served to the guests on spits. Knives are to be seen scattered

A royal table: the wedding feast of Matilda (daughter of Henry I) and the Emperor Henry V

Meat served on spits

about the table, but no forks: fingers, as for many centuries after, performed their natural function. Therefore washing of hands before and after meals was customary. Dishes seem to have been shared, one dish between two diners. Bones and the less edible portions of meat or fish could be thrown on the floor for the dogs. In the ground-floor halls which predominated in Anglo-Saxon England and were again in favour in the twelfth century, beggars could often wander in and would, literally, get the crumbs from the rich man's table.

This description of domestic life applies also to the households of the great barons and, much simplified, to the lesser baronage. For the difference was of degree rather than of kind. Involved in the lives of these high-ranking alien lords were the lives of a

The beggar at the feast

far greater number of low-ranking natives. These were the domestic servants, who ate at the lords' expense and many of whom would have no homes of their own. From the point of view of food, they must have been better off than their social equals in other walks of life, but their living conditions in castle or manor or on the road were probably indescribable. They lived where and how they could. The number of these people whose lives were closely bound up with the new aristocracy must have been very considerable.

46

Our principal authority for the dress worn in the eleventh century is the Bayeux Tapestry, which has the great advantage of showing us English and Norman fashions. The main difference seems to be in hair styles. The English wore their hair longish at the back (*see* p. 6) and moustaches or beards according to age. The Normans wore their hair cut short at the back and their faces appear in the embroidery as clean-shaven,

Eleventh-century armour

although, given the shaving equipment available at the time, shaving was probably indifferently close, quite painful and certainly not a daily occurrence.

The Tapestry has, of course, many pictures of men in armour, both Norman and English, and the differences are not great. The main garment was a hauberk of chain mail, about knee length, slit up the cruck, with elbow-length sleeves and a reinforcing square of mail over the chest. The hauberk was extended at the back into a fitting hood, which covered the head and neck.

The couched lance, twelfth century

This basic garment was of the simplest shape as can be seen in pictures of the armour being carried on poles. It required two men to carry one hauberk, so it must have been heavy. In battle, a conical helmet with nose piece would be worn, elbow-length mail gloves and for the highest leaders mailed leg coverings laced up the back. Most men, however, wore the puttee-like hose of civilian dress. An older type of armour, still worn, consisted of a canvas or leather jerkin, sewn all over with lozenge-shaped metal plates. All carried wooden shields, mostly kite-shaped, with a strap on the inner side making it possible to sling the shield round the neck, leaving both arms free. Some of the English shields were round. A few were painted, although true heraldic designs do not appear until much later. The weapons were spears, maces and the two-handed axe for the English, and swords, spears and maces for the Normans. The leaders had a pennon flying at the top of the lance. The Normans fought on horseback, the English on foot (*see* p. 22), and although the use of the stirrup made it possible to couch a lance few of the Normans seem to have followed this technique at Hastings. In the next century the couched lance was almost obligatory. Armour changed little over most of the period. It

48

was not until the end of the twelfth century that the flat-topped helmet appeared with a detachable ventail which protected the jaw and throat. At this time also a surcoat of linen or silk was often worn over the armour. This may have been an outcome of crusading warfare. The eastern sun, beating down on uncovered metal, could turn armour into an oven for its wearer! Poorer knights and barons were still wearing in 1200 the styles of 1066, for chain mail was expensive and it wore well, if rust could be kept at bay.

The civilian dress was much the same for both Norman and English of the same social class. One presumes that a shirt and *braies* (wide-bottomed breeches) were worn under the knee-length tunic. On top of this, men of rank wore a short mantle, a straight length of material fastened with a brooch on the right shoulder. Priests were indistinguishable from laymen except by their tonsure. Kings on their thrones wore more dignified garments, with longer tunic and mantle and, in Edward's case, embroidered bands on the tunic. Probably the state robes of a king were of fine material, richly embroidered. At any rate we know that, when William first visited his duchy after his English coronation, his Norman subjects were very much impressed by the clothes he had acquired in England. Civilian attire changed over the period more than armour. The Normans seem to have taken to the longer hair-styles of the English and, under William II, to have carried them to extremes,

Crusader, late twelfth century, showing surcoat and helmet with ventail

49

Battle scene, late twelfth century. Note little change in armour or peasant dress since the eleventh century

young men wearing their hair long and curled and often sporting beards. They also wore much longer garments, making athletic exercise difficult, and shoes with long points stuffed with wool. The fashion was regarded by the older men and by the clergy as effeminate and degenerate, and the licentiousness of William II was blamed, although, if Orderic Vitalis is to be believed, it was not confined to England, but could be seen all over western Europe. There was reaction in the later part of Henry I's reign and clothes became more functional, except on state occasions when full-length robes were worn. The main garments throughout the twelfth century were the breeches, a tunic of silk or linen with long sleeves (often detachable) and a surcoat, or chlamys, with three-quarter sleeves, getting longer as the century progressed. Over this in cold weather was worn a pelisse lined with fur, with no sleeves or very wide ones, and in still colder weather the whole might be surmounted by a mantle fastening either at the centre front or on the right shoulder. This could be edged with fur or even lined with ermine. Women wore the same as their menfolk, but without the braies, and their garments were always long, and the mantle was fastened at the centre front. In the twelfth century the robes became more flowing and the sleeves became wider, in some cases so extravagantly wide that they had to be knotted up. Tunics were girdled twice round the waist, with the ends of the girdle falling down the centre front. Women wore their hair in long braided plaits.

The fur-lined garments, which were so necessary a part of the medieval wardrobe, possibly even more for the cold and draughty interiors than for the great outdoors, were often part of the livery of the servants of great households and particularly of the royal household. Hats were worn indoors as well as out. On the other hand both sexes seem to have gone naked to bed, a fact which accounts for the rich fur-lined coverlets, which were common among the wealthy. Book illustrations of the period show kings and queens in bed in their birthday suits, but wearing crowns to show their rank.

Female costume: wide sleeves

William the Conqueror was, as Duke of Normandy, a tenant and a subject of the King of France, albeit he was more powerful than his suzerain and sovereign. His court was a replica of that of the French king and on a smaller scale his own tenants and subjects—the terms were almost synonymous in a feudal age—had similar households and similar officers. It is not unlikely that, in participating in his enterprise in 1066, they hoped and indeed expected to hold positions in England equivalent to that of their duke in France. They were to be disappointed for, except during the 19 years of Stephen's reign, the kings of the Norman and Angevin dynasties managed to combine a strong feudal position with the non-feudal English tradition of kingship and to retain political power in their own hands. This did not prevent their chief

Curtained bed and occupants

barons reproducing in their own lives and habits the charac-
teristics we have already associated with the king. They had
their chancellors, stewards, constables, marshals and the rest,
but, as the king denied them political independence, these officers
remained purely domestic. They moved round the country from
estate to estate. They had their castles and, like the king, they
gradually converted parts of the timber structures to stone—
either a stone keep as at Bridgnorth or a curtain wall with a
rectangular gatehouse, like that built by Count Alan of Brittany
at Richmond in Yorkshire.

When William became king of England he claimed to be the
ultimate landlord of every square inch of English soil, and the
circumstances of the Conquest gave him actual control of a large
proportion of it. The Church kept its land, about one-quarter
of the country, and the king retained in his own hands about
another quarter. The rest he was prepared to use to reward his
followers and at the same time to secure for himself a feudal
army of about 5,000 mounted soldiers. Until the great Domesday
Survey was made in 1086 (and William died in 1087) the king
had no means of knowing how much land he really had and what
sort of return could be expected from it. It must have seemed to

Richmond, Yorkshire: curtain wall with rectangular gatehouse

him almost inexhaustible. What he did was to grant lands to his greater followers and to confirm lands to the principal churches on condition that they maintained so many men, the number varying from one to 60 and based on a purely arbitrary assessment. The tenants-in-chief contracted to serve themselves, with their quota of warriors, armed and equipped; to perform castle guard at the king's castles; and to give the king counsel when called upon. There were certain incidental profits which the king could make from his tenants and they from theirs. A good tenant would always be willing to aid his lord in times of need. This could be translated into pecuniary terms. It came to be recognised as right and proper for a king or other lord to demand an 'aid', that is a sum of money, from his tenants on the occasion of the knighting of his eldest son, the first marriage of his eldest daughter and the ransoming of the lord himself should that be necessary. Richard I was the only king who needed ransom money, when he was captured on his return from the Third Crusade. Lords did, in fact, expect aid from their tenants on other occasions, as when they got into the clutches of Jewish moneylenders (charging more than 40 per cent a year!). When a tenant died, the heir had to pay a relief to the lord for the recognition of his right to succeed.

Among other perquisites of lordship were rights of wardship and marriage. An heir under age was in the guardianship not of his mother or relations but of his lord who, with the reservation that he must maintain the heir according to his estate, had the right to draw the revenues from the property. It also became usual for him to arrange the marriage of the infant, which could be a profitable right if many fathers of marriageable daughters were interested. As regards heiresses, they owed service of marriage throughout their lives. Fifty was a good old age for men, and most died younger either in battle or of disease. A girl, married in childhood, might be free to marry many times and each time she was widowed she would have a right to dower for life, which was a factor to be considered by prospective suitors and therefore increased her 'market' value to her lord. There exists, by chance, a record covering twelve shires in the year 1185—*The Roll of Ladies, Boys and Girls in the King's gift.*

It gives details of estates, and in the case of women their complete marital history, to enable the king's officers to exact the highest price for the wardship or marriage.

The warriors, whose service the tenants-in-chief owed, were called in the Latin documents of the time *milites*. The English called them *cnihts*, a term implying a kind of upper servant. They were, in effect, trained men-at-arms, and so most of them remained in the first decades after 1066, when every alien lord had to be prepared at all times to defend himself or his king. This meant that lords had either to farm out their manors or put them in the hands of bailiffs. The time came when it seemed less necessary to have soldiers always at the ready, and gradually a proportion of these professional soldiers was settled on the land, each getting one or more manors in lieu of keep in his lord's hall. This settling of the cnihts on the land gave them a very different standing in the country. The knight was now in the place of the Anglo-Saxon thegn. He was the squire. This development was

Channel crossing for men and horses

carried a step further in the twelfth century, when the king showed himself more and more willing to accept a money payment in lieu of knight service. With this scutage or shield money he could hire mercenaries in France, where most of his fighting took place, and he was not troubled by the enormous task of conveying horses and men across the Channel, nor was he limited in his journey and campaign to the 40 days which was customary for compulsory military service. Until inflation hit the country in the later years of the twelfth century, and the cost of keeping a knight and his attendant in the field rose from 8*d.* to 2*s.*, or even 3*s.*, a day, the king was probably better off for the change. For a good many knights scutage meant a revolution in their way of life. They became increasingly identified with the land. They took more and more part in local government and in the developing judicial system of the twelfth century, and they were unconsciously preparing themselves to form an important element in Parliament, when it gradually took shape in the thirteenth century. Not the whole of the knightly class was demilitarised. That part which was not was still encompassed in the lives of the king and barons, described in this chapter. The rest ceased more or less to be part of the baronial households and must be identified with village life.

Further Reading

D. M. Stenton, *English Society in the Early Middle Ages* (Pelican)
F. M. Stenton, *English Feudalism 1066–1166*
R. A. Brown, *English Medieval Castles*
See also Stenton, Douglas and Brooke (p. 24)

III

The Village

In 1066 Domesday Book was ordered. With the exception of certain towns, which were separately surveyed, the impression is of a predominantly agricultural society. The Commissioners were instructed to find out about each manor 'how many hides there are; how many ploughs in demesne and how many belonging to the men; how many villeins, how many cottars; how many sokemen; how much woodland; how much meadow; how much pasture; how many mills; how many fisheries; . . .' The king wanted to know the answers for three separate dates: in King Edward's time, when King William gave it and now, that is in 1086. The very form of the questionnaire shows that, whatever the social and legal position of the men who actually worked the land, they and the food they produced were the basis of life. The feudal king might reckon his power in terms of military service owed to him, but a succession of bad harvests could result in famine and pestilence and bring the whole might of the kingdom low. The Normans did not bring with them new agricultural methods. These were the time-honoured ones we have seen in use in the Anglo-Saxon village, changing only very slowly over the centuries. The Anglo-Saxon geneats, geburs, cottars and slaves became, in Domesday Book, the freemen, sokemen, villeins, cottars and slaves. Gradually, in the decades after 1066, the tendency was for the free geburs, and sometimes even the geneats, to slip down the social ladder, to be lumped together as 'villeins', which really meant no more than villagers, but which came in time to imply a legal as well as an economic

56

Domesday Book: a passage from the first page for Wiltshire

lack of freedom. On the other hand there was an upgrading of the actual slave class. There were some 25,000 slaves entered in Domesday, but the numbers gradually diminished as those slaves who had their own hovels and worked on the land became absorbed into the great class of the semi-free. But although these changes in status did have some practical consequences, which will be mentioned later, what affected the villager most was the attitude of the stranger, in both custom and language, to whom he now owed rent and service.

The soldiery of William in 1066 were, as has been said before, fortune hunters. The greatest of them held fantastic stretches of land. Roger of Montgomery held large portions of Sussex, Surrey and Hampshire and many estates in Wiltshire, Middlesex, Hertfordshire, Gloucestershire, Cambridgeshire, Warwickshire and Staffordshire, as well as his chief holding, some seven-eighths of Shropshire. He kept the best part, one fifth of the whole in extent, though only a little under half in value, in demesne. The remainder he let out to tenants, but he also farmed out many of his demesne manors at rents well above those at which they were assessed in Domesday. If the middlemen were to make a profit, and they intended to, they had to be very keen taskmasters. We find every item of estate management put to

57

A mill (note lack of perspective)

account, from the Church to which all must pay tithe, to the mill at which they must grind their corn and the lord's bakery at which they must bake their bread, all, of course, in return for a proportion of the corn and the bread. They must fold their sheep in the lord's fold and so provide him with the manure so badly needed. Some of these things were taken for granted by the villagers. Others they seemed to resent. One of the obligations which they apparently tried to evade, sometimes successfully, was that of grinding their corn at the lord's mill. After all, a couple of hand querns behind one's cottage would do the job easily. It was just an added chore for the housewife.

Even after the Conquest there were some parts of England which were less manorialised than others. This was the case particularly in the north and in parts of the Danelaw. There were also manors where there was no demesne and the villagers farmed the whole themselves, giving their rent in money or in kind and owing no labour services. This happened on some of the manors belonging to St Paul's. Willesden was one of these manors. The Canons of St Paul's were a really go-ahead group. Some of their manors they leased to farmers. On these they provided the most up-to-date domestic and farm buildings and equipment and they stocked the manors with grain and other necessaries, for all of which they expected a return in increased rent—and they got it. One manor, so leased, started at £5 per annum and increased by £1 annually. Another ecclesiastical landlord had no use for the farmer or middleman. Abbot Samson of St Edmund's according to Jocelyn of Brakelonde, one of his monks, felt that he could get better results by keeping the manors in his own hands.

He was no sluggard and began before all else to build barns and byres: and he was more especially eager to cultivate his lands with profit, and was also vigilant in looking after his woods, concerning the granting and diminishing of which he confessed himself most avaricious. One sole manor, that of Thorp, he confirmed by charter to a certain Englishman, an adscript to the soil [i.e. he was a villein, not a freeman!] in whose faithfulness he had all the greater confidence, because he was a good farmer and could speak no French.

This was near the end of the twelfth century. Does it mean that a consciousness of English nationality was beginning to develop? Samson himself was accustomed to preach in the Norfolk dialect.

Sometimes the lord of the manor was not resident. Abbot Samson could not have been. He would then put a steward in charge and, if the steward had many manors to supervise, he might visit each one not more than twice a year. He would arrive with his train of clerks and servants and upset the life of the manor while he inspected the accounts on behalf of his lord. Many of the servants would be quartered on the villagers. In this case the local officer of the lord would be the bailiff, who might occupy a very simple manor house and run several adjacent manors. The lord's interests in the labour of the villagers were taken care of by the reeve, usually one of the villeins, elected by his fellows or appointed by the lord or bailiff. The job was an unenviable one, even though it carried with it some privileges and exemption from actual physical labour in the field. It was the reeve who decided on which days the lord's ploughing or harvesting work should be done, and he saw to it that the work was not scamped. The freeman owed no ploughing service, but the villein had not only to do the work, but he and his fellows had to provide the plough and the plough-team and the seed. The plough-team of Domesday Book is an eight-ox team, and clearly this type of plough must have been in common use on many of the great open fields. In fact, the long, waving ridges, still preserved on land which has been pasture for centuries, represent the swerve of the cumbrous eight-ox plough. But the illustrations of ploughs

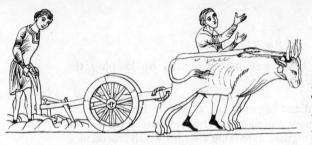

Two-ox plough team

in early manuscripts and in the Bayeux Tapestry represent the plough with one, two or four animals, never eight. The documentary evidence refers to an eight- or six-ox team, but there is a Domesday entry for Yorkshire: 'One villein is there ploughing with two oxen'. His was hardly likely to be the only two-ox team in England. There must have been villages where the soil was more suited to a lighter plough or where the physical features made an eight-ox team impossible. The ox was the best plough animal in that he was cheaper to feed than a horse, that he was stronger and that his flesh could be used for food when his working days were over. Eating of horse flesh was forbidden by the Church. However, horses were faster than oxen, and in any case such was the difficulty in finding winter feed for animals that ploughmen could not be too fussy. In the agricultural market at Smithfield in the late twelfth century 'mares fit for the plough' were offered for sale.

Most landlords, however, were conservative and, except that they were more insistent on their rights and that more and more of the peasantry found themselves burdened with services and obligations which were the badges of servitude, what was said in the first chapter on the agricultural régime applies equally after the Conquest. In some few cases labour services would have been commuted for a money payment, but the great movement in this

Four-ox plough team

direction was to come in the later thirteenth and the fourteenth centuries. One obligation, which was usually considered as the hallmark of the unfree, was the payment of *merchet*, a fine paid to the lord for permission for a villein's daughter to marry. This question of marriage particularly interested the lord if the girl was to marry a man from another manor, in which case her offspring would be lost to the lord. There were also complications if she wanted to marry a freeman, because her offspring would be free. In a small and self-contained community like the village, in which freemen and villeins lived and worked side by side and were often as rich or as poor as one another (witness the villein to whom Abbot Samson entrusted the manor of Thorp), this case must often have occurred. It and other problems were discussed and settled when the court of the manor met, either in the hall of the manor house, hence the name 'court' for some of our country mansions, or in other convenient places in the open. Intermarriage between quite distant relations was forbidden by the Church, to within seven degrees—counting brothers as one degree and cousins as two—until 1216. Obviously these regulations must have been a dead letter in an interrelated village. If we had records we should probably see the results of such inbreeding in village idiots, such as are found in isolated communities even today. There were numbers of these about in our period and they were often regarded as sources of entertainment by their more fortunate brothers.

If the squire was forward-looking and his tenants enterprising, it was possible for some of them to carve out small holdings for themselves on the wasteland or unwanted woodland. This involved clearing the land and preparing it for cultivation, a backbreaking task with the primitive tools of the time, but it was by this means that the landscape of England was gradually being changed in the twelfth century. The isolated homestead could easily be the forerunner of a new village community, which might have its open fields, but was more likely to have enclosed areas, brought under the plough by the pioneers.

Neither the Norman Conquest nor the passing of the centuries made any difference to the hovel which housed the poorest members of the village community. It remained the simplest

Framework of a cruck building

structure which would provide shelter from the elements and which could be erected without outside help. Its frame could vary from two pairs of branches lashed together at the top and supporting a ridge pole to two poles sunk in the ground, also supporting a ridge pole. The ridge pole itself would provide support for other timbers, the feet of which would be fixed in the ground or in a low wall of mud or a solid foundation plank, which would give rectangular floor space. The roof timbers would be covered with turves (grass inside), mud or thatch. The low wall was not to give height but to prevent the outward thrust of the roof. Any headroom must be gained by excavating the floor. An improvement on this was the cruck dwelling. The cruck was an oak branch, suitably bent. This was split to form identical halves, which were then set upright and joined at the top. If a suitable branch could be found for the other end the two could be joined by a ridge pole. Additional length could be obtained by adding further pairs of crucks and further ridge poles, to make the type of long house which would accommodate the family at one end and the cattle at the other. The pole became more or less standard length and the rod, pole or perch had its place in our tables of measurement until quite recently. The biggest break-through in timber-frame building was probably the collar, a horizontal beam joining the crucks below the crest. This added enormously to the rigidity of the structure, as it lessened the thrust of the roof and made side walls possible. Another step forward was a horizontal beam at the bend of the crucks but extended beyond to meet upright posts joined to the feet of the crucks. These beams and posts,

62

connected by other beams and posts, provided the framework for a simple house with walls. The framework and the gable ends would be filled in with lighter timbers and with wattle and daub, a pattern of uprights woven with flexible branches, withies or rushes and then plastered on both sides, usually simultaneously, with a kind of mud concrete (mud reinforced with hair, straw or manure). Another method, which allowed the width of the building to be increased, was to plant two rows of upright posts supporting the roof timbers at their junction with the collars. This produced the aisled hall, which left the centre of the hall clear, while the space between the posts could be used as animal stalls, sleeping quarters for humans or, in important halls, service alleys. This gives the whole range of village houses in wood, and, with the addition of whitewash, they probably looked quite picturesque.

The peasant's house might be a one-chamber structure, or, if long enough, it could have a wattle-and-daub partition, giving a small sleeping room. The floor would be of earth, and the straw, rushes or furze, which provided the bedding, would give little protection against frozen earth or the seeping damp of a thaw. Rheumatism and arthritis must have been common ailments. The smoke from the wood or turf fire in the living compartment would find its way out through chinks in the roof or through the door. Unless some penthouse shanty could be provided the few animals might have to share the living room. Better-off villagers would increase the length of their houses and the cattle would be housed at one end, the family having to pass through this end to reach its own quarters. The next stage would be to make a storage loft in the roof space. Finally the animals would be banished to farm buildings and the house reserved for human occupation and such domestic livestock as fowls, dogs and pigs.

Harold's house at Bosham

The manor house almost certainly had a chamber for its lord and lady, either partitioned off one end of the hall or in a separate building. All these degrees of housing existed before the Conquest and might all be found in any one village at any one time. The Bayeux Tapestry even depicts two-storey dwellings, but how they were built with the carpentering techniques available it is difficult to say. An imaginative reconstruction of a royal palace, recently excavated at Cheddar in Somerset, gives us some idea of what the owner of a manor house might aim at, although he would not need such a large house as a king

Reconstruction of the Saxon Palace at Cheddar, tenth century

of Wessex. A still more recent excavation at No. 10 Downing Street, during alterations there, brought to light evidence of what was probably a large farm or manor house. The finds suggested a barnlike building and it is probably to old-fashioned barns that we should turn for a visual image of the domestic environment of the better-off countryman.

No description exists of the life of the villager in the eleventh and twelfth centuries, but it must have been, by our standards, brutish and hard. The menfolk would be out in the fields or

about their special occu-
pations soon after day-
break, having broken
their fast briefly with
coarse rye bread, washed
down with a watery ale.
The womenfolk would
look after the children
and the animals, milk the
cows and ewes and make
cheese, from the skimmed
cow's milk and ewe's
milk. Six to ten ewes
would produce as much as

Barn at Godmersham: early form of timber aisled hall

one cow. They would prepare the great pot for the evening meal,
which would generally consist of bread and a meatless soup.
Fresh meat was available only in the autumn, when all the animals, other than those needed for the plough or for breeding,
were slaughtered, owing to the scarcity of winter feeding. In
any case the medieval sheep and pig were very much smaller
than their modern successors. The great virtue of the pig was
that he could feed himself. Rarely was any effort made to fatten
him up for the table. If there was any quantity of such meat it
would be salted down for occasional use at winter feasts. If
there was no salt it would be hung in the rafters above the fire
and the smoke would both preserve it and ward off the flies.
Fresh or salted, it must have been leathery in the extreme and
often overripe for eating. Apart from the difficulty of roasting
at the one all-purpose fire, the meat was more suited to boiling.

Slaughtering animals and boiling meat

Pot for boiling, with spits above

In medieval pictures of roasting, the spits are usually loaded with birds, not the flesh of quadrupeds.

All villages, except perhaps some upland mining villages, must have been mainly self-supporting. However, the manor house might buy flax for producing the linen for the napery and special-occasion tunics of the lord and his family, and their robes might be bought at the nearest fair. In addition certain articles had to be bought if they were not produced locally. Salt, tar, iron bought in four-pound bars, millstones, steel for tipping the edges of instruments and possibly cloth for use in the dairy, grange and malthouse were the most important. The centres which produced these would have a value over and above their value as agricultural land. When the king and the other lords, who were lucky enough to have rights in the great salt *wiches*, Droitwich, Northwich, Middlewich, Nantwich, had fulfilled their own needs, the 'salter' moved in, with his waggon, his pack animals or even his own back. He paid the appropriate toll and took his precious commodity to the market towns within travelling distance of the saltpans. The custom had not entirely died out at the beginning of this century, when the salt waggon was a familiar sight in the west Midlands and the bonneted saltwoman sold her blocks of salt to the housewife, to be stored and then ground for general use. Fish was another commodity, localised in its incidence and much in demand especially during Lent. This could give a special character to the vills and manors where it was available. Great lords were willing enough to take their manorial tribute in herrings—tens of thousands of them!

It was probably in winter time, when people were kept indoors, that many of the incidental chores, for both men and women, must have been done, and very unpleasant it must have been in the dark, odorous and smoky conditions of the interior, with artificial light only from the fire and from the rushlights made by the women. The men made the wooden platters and spoons which were the staple domestic equipment and most of the rough tools needed in cultivation, scythes, rakes, etc. They plaited osiers and reeds into baskets and 'weeles' for catching fish, and made flails from holly or thorn, fastened with thongs to staves. The women spun and wove the wool from the family sheep, made the poor man's linen from hemp or nettles and sewing thread also from nettles. They also plaited straw or reeds for neck collars. They peeled rushes, which they then soaked in fat for their rushlights. There was almost certainly an alehouse (house of potation) in each village, run by an alewife. At least, the alewife was a common character in the thirteenth century and often in trouble at the manor court for brewing ale of inferior quality or for selling it above the legal price. In summer one imagines that, apart from the necessity of putting in long hours at work, it must have been a relief to be out of doors as much as possible, with the village green as the local dance hall and wrestling floor.

Apart from the village green and the manor house, there was another centre of life in the village and that was the church. The church touched life at all points. In the first place it was concerned with baptism, marriage and burial, and one gets the impression that the most important of these from the Church's point of view was burial, with its fees (soulscot). The law about Christian marriage was still in a state of flux in the twelfth century, and the Church, particularly the porch, was still probably as important as a public place where the contract could be witnessed as it was as the scene of a sacrament. Betrothal was almost as binding as marriage. But there were other church services, especially the Mass, and the parishioners would be expected

Wrestling

67

Milburn, Westmorland: village with houses arranged round a green

to attend whenever possible on the many feast days, although it is doubtful whether such attendance would be allowed to interfere with the daily round, and it is possible that the congregation consisted more of women than of men. There was no seating and the congregation stood, as it still does in the churches of the Orthodox communion. Churches were painted inside, often crudely no doubt, but the paintings told part of the Bible story or the life of the patron saint to a people which was completely illiterate. Certain boys of the village would be used by the priest as acolytes and it is probably among these that we should find those sons of villeins who applied in the manor court for permission to enter the priesthood. Once this was granted the aspirant might go far. It seems certain that Robert Grosseteste, first Chancellor of Oxford University at the end of our period, later Bishop of Lincoln and one of the foremost scholars of the thirteenth century, was the son of a villein.

But the church and the churchyard served other purposes than purely religious ones. The church might be the scene of the village meeting. It might also be used for jollification on holidays, including dancing, although rowdyism was frowned on by the ecclesiastical authorities. The churchyard was frequently used in the Middle Ages for buying and selling, although this was more likely in towns than in villages. Such surplus stock as existed would generally be taken to the nearest market town on market days, and the happy owner would be able to supplement his family's meagre rations or buy such equipment or clothing as could not be made in the village.

On the whole, however, the eleventh- and twelfth-century village was an enclosed community, sometimes increasing its communal fields at the expense of the fringing wasteland, sometimes throwing out a new community through the enterprise of young peasants and the far-sighted co-operation of the lord of the manor or his local representative. The village met the central government at certain points and the connection was to increase as time went on. William I had taken over and modified

Woman with two betrothed: the discarded suitor won't give up!

a pre-Conquest custom that the peasantry and the lower orders in towns should be grouped in tens from the age of 12 onwards, the numbers being very liberally interpreted to cover a whole manor or village. Each group, under its own elected leader, would be responsible for reporting any breach of the law by one of its members. The system was further linked to a developing national system in 1166, when Henry II decreed that 12 men of a hundred, founding their reports on the statements of the chief men of the tithings, should, twice a year, accuse before the sheriff all those who had committed certain crimes. These suspects would be sent for trial before the King's Justices. In such a way the villages were to be drawn into a national network.

Further Reading

P. Vinogradoff, *Villeinage in England*
R. Lennard, *Rural England, 1086–1134*, 1959
C. S. and C. S. Orwin, *The Open Fields* (2nd ed.), 1954
A. L. Poole, *Obligations of Society in the XII and XIII Centuries*, 1946
W. G. Hoskins, *The Making of the English Landscape*, 1955
M. W. Beresford and J. K. S. St. Joseph, *Medieval England: an aerial survey*

IV

The Town

In the days of the old English kingdom the boroughs were, in a very real sense, the king's boroughs. They lived under his special protection, or peace, and the borough and market dues and the toll payable on merchandise either went to augment the king's revenues or were divided two to one between the king and the earl. After the Norman Conquest, the then-existing boroughs continued as before to be regarded as the king's and he claimed the right to tallage, that is to tax, them at will, as he could his demesne manors. But change was in the air. Whether from a desire to share in the profits from commerce, or for the convenience of having commercial goods available on their own door-steps or even as a prestige symbol, the feudal lords of the Norman era wanted to plant boroughs on their own estates. In the case of a great abbey there was usually no need to plant. The employment available in a monastery and the unusual reservoir of custom provided by an enormous household, permanently resident in one place, meant that towns grew up naturally on monastic estates. In the case of some boroughs, like Chester, Leicester, Warwick and Reading, the Norman kings transferred their rights to barons or, in the case of Reading, to Henry I's new foundation, Reading Abbey.

If you were a feudal lord and wanted a town or borough on your land, the first step was to obtain from the king the right to hold a market. After that much would depend on the means at your disposal. If you were a rich and powerful lord, you could lay out a site with streets and building plots. You could build churches. You could then invite prospective burgesses to take up the plots at the usual rent of one shilling per annum, paid quarterly. Some agricultural land outside the walls was usually attached to the borough, but it was never sufficient to provide for the needs of the town and in some cases only a small number of the burgesses worked the land, but the organisation of the agricultural routine belonged to the burgesses acting as a community. To set up a borough of this type meant risking a good deal of capital and many would-be town-builders would not have the wherewithal. If you were of that number, you would, after making sure of your market, set aside land for development. This might easily be an extension of an existing village and the new freeholds would grow up alongside the villein crofts of the original manor. Such a borough would have little or no planning and, unless it happened to be particularly well sited for trading, it might have no future. The simplest form of layout for a borough was the triangular one, formed by the intersection of two converging roads, often with the church and churchyard forming the short side of this very acute-angled triangle. The original building plots would line the two long sides of the triangle and the open space in the middle would be for market stalls, temporary at first, although they tended to become permanent shops in time. This plan was adopted in a number of pre-Conquest towns and can sometimes be traced today on the maps of their modern descendants. More complicated, and apparently a

post-Conquest development, was the grid plan, with streets crossing each other more or less at right angles and allowing for rectangular blocks, which could be divided into building lots or used for a church or a market place. One early example is Bury St Edmunds, which was the result of a planned expansion of the old town by Abbot Baldwin soon after the Conquest. More than a century later, in

71

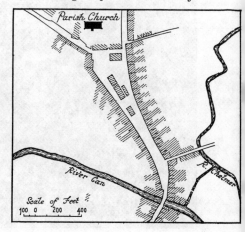

Triangular-plan town: Chelmsford

fact a few years after our period closes, Richard le Poore, Bishop of Salisbury, deliberately deserted Old Sarum in 1220 and planned a new town on his own church lands. The present Salisbury Cathedral was sited between the new town and the River Avon.

One of the attractions of England for Duke William was its wealth, and that wealth was in part derived from a flourishing trade. Even in the Confessor's time the Emperor's men and the men of Rouen had quays in London. English cloth and English cheeses, to name but two products, had been well known on the Continent for a long time. English cheeses again, with other agricultural products, were welcome in Norway, where the configuration of the land made agriculture a minor industry. In return Norwegian fish was welcome in English markets. The Norman Conquest meant a temporary setback in trading figures, mainly for political reasons.

The boroughs also suffered a temporary setback. Some, like York, Chester and Stafford, were devastated during William's punitive expedition to the north and west of England in 1069–70. Chester, in the time of the Confessor, had 487 houses paying tax.

Bury St Edmunds, Suffolk, as planned by Abbot Baldwin soon after 1066: grid plan, with main streets parallel to the abbey frontage

In 1086 there were 205 less. In other cases the boroughs, particularly the shire towns, suffered from William's policy of planting a castle in the best strategic position. He was as ruthless as the modern town-planner and any houses on ground wanted for his castles were just pulled down. A rod and hook would do the job! Domesday Book says of Lincoln that in the time of King Edward there were 970 inhabited houses in the city. When Domesday was compiled in 1086 there were 240 less. Of these '166 were destroyed on account of the castle. The remaining 74 are waste outside the castle, not because of the oppression of the sheriff and officers, but by reason of misfortune and poverty and the ravage of fires.' This same sentence, with differing figures,

Pictorialised diagram of Salisbury, Wiltshire, as planned by Bishop Richard le Poore in 1220

could probably be written for a score of other towns. Bridlington in Yorkshire declined from a taxable value of £32 to one of eight shillings.

Then too William did not trust the English boroughs. Here were concentrations of people who might easily plot against the new ruler. One answer was the castle. Another was the settlement of French burgesses in what was often a new burghal community side by side with the old, but having its own court parallel to the English borough court, sharing the market rights and having many privileges, such as exemption from the borough tax. Ultimately the two communities would merge, but in the twelfth century the English eyed their new neighbours with no friendly eye, complaining, as at Shrewsbury, that they were expected to pay the same tax as before, although 51 houses had been destroyed for the castle, 50 were waste, 59 had been given by the Earl to his new abbey and the French community occupied houses free of tax which had formerly been tax-paying. As the tax was imposed on the borough as a whole, this naturally increased the burden on the remaining tax-paying burgesses.

But the setback in trade and town development was temporary. The Conquest was accepted and the towns, with their promise of wealth, became the favoured protégés of king, Church and barons alike, who were willing to grant them charters of privilege in the hope of increased populations and increased profits. The Norman barons, although they did not follow the old English habit of maintaining town houses, yet bought town sites for re-selling or letting. William I's brother, the Count of Mortain, had 14 houses in York, as well as the Church of Holy Cross and two stalls in the Shambles. The Normans had a keen eye for a good business proposition!

The rapid expansion of trade all over Europe in the twelfth century, particularly during the second half, meant that English towns were flourishing. Bristol, with open access to the sea yet sufficiently inland to be comparatively safe from pirate attack, grew rapidly. It became a port of call for Norwegian traders on their way via the Hebrides to western Europe and when the accession of Henry II, husband of the Duchess of Aquitaine, brought that great wine-growing region within the ambit of English trade, Bristol became a natural depot for wines from Bordeaux. The Anglo-Normans gave up their attempt to drink the inferior stuff, which was all that could be made from grapes grown in the inclement English climate, and settled for the wines of the Bordeaux region, as they have continued to do to the present day. The Aquitainian wine-growers, with a ready market, turned their cornlands into vineyards and bought English agricultural produce with the profits of their wine trade, to the mutual advantage of English and Aquitainian producers.

In general, however, the greatest ports, and therefore the greatest towns, were those which had ready access by water to the east and south coasts. The east coast attracted traders from Flanders and the north German towns. The 'men of Cologne' were everywhere. One flourishing port in the twelfth century was Lynn, now King's Lynn, through which passed the surplus agricultural produce of the Bishop of Ely's manors, and to a lesser degree that of the Abbeys of Ramsay and Crowland, and the woolclip of the Fenland sheep. Archaeologists working in King's Lynn have had some interesting finds and more may yet come to light. They include a wooden wharf, which is provisionally dated as thirteenth century or earlier, and which shows, among other things, that the Great Ouse flowed about 60 yards east of its present course.

Part of the early medieval wharf at King's Lynn, Norfolk, uncovered in 1964

The wharf is apparently the first of its type to be found in Britain, but closely resembles wharves of the same period at Bergen in Norway and Staveren in the Low Countries, with which places trade links would be very possible.

How did life in these eleventh- and twelfth-century towns differ from that of the villages and manors of the period? Clearly there would be great differences between town and town. The smaller ones, often not so big as a modern English village, would not differ greatly, except in their market, from the villages. The larger towns, those with 4,000 or more inhabitants, would be more urban in character. Comparatively few people would be actively engaged in agricultural work, but in some of the boroughs, particularly those belonging to the greater abbeys, old manorial customs still existed. The burgesses had to grind their corn at the lord's mill and bake their bread in his ovens. Some might even be subject to the payment of merchet for marrying their daughters.

If a town had a royal castle there would be a rota of barons, with their knights, performing castle guard. Some of these barons would maintain houses in the town or, as in the case of Newcastle-upon-Tyne, in the bailey of the castle. There would be a varying population of priests. Norwich, admittedly well off in this respect, boasted 20 churches and 43 chapels in 1086. The major part of the town's population, however, would consist of merchants, craftsmen who both made and sold goods, their apprentices, journeymen assistants and unskilled artisans. These last were recruited in some degree from deserters from manors, who hoped to obtain their freedom by breathing the free air of a borough for a year and a day. In some towns, such as Leicester, the merchants were organised into gilds, important enough to play a big part in the government of the borough. In others, the crafts were organised in the twelfth century and such craft gilds were, in twentieth-century terminology, closed shops. They supervised the training of apprentices, the quality and price of goods produced, the wages paid to journeymen, and they acted also as welfare groups, looking after their members in sickness and misfortune.

The original building sites in the boroughs, particularly planned boroughs, tended to be large, with a frontage of some 40–60 feet and with a considerable depth behind, so permitting the building of a country-type house, with hall, solar and out-buildings, courtyards and even gardens. Some plots might retain this rural aspect but the vast increase in trade made land in the more prosperous towns a commodity with a scarcity value. As a characteristic of a burgage tenement was that its owner could dispose of it freely, we find the lots being subdivided and the houses packed together, with a narrow frontage to the street. In the eleventh century all, and in the twelfth almost all, the houses would be of wood. In a typical merchant's or substantial crafts-man's house the ground floor facing the street would be the shop or workshop. Behind would be the hall, the main room and living quarters of the household. Above the shop would be the solar, the family room. Some houses had only one room down and one up, which latter would be an all-purpose room. The shop space might be subdivided, one half being let to another merchant, who would live in a different part of the town. The shops themselves, some as small as six feet by 15 feet, were not so much places of sale as workshops where goods were made to order. The casual selling was done

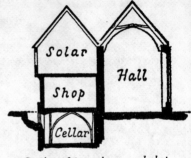

Section of town house and shop

on market day, either in a market square or in booths set up in the centre of a specially wide street, like Broad Street in Oxford. The market was therefore very much an integral part of the life of a town, which would go to great lengths, including violence, to prevent the grant of another market within an area which it regarded as its selling ground. As today, the market was held on a fixed day each week and a favourite day was Sunday. In spite of the fulminations of the Church, towns were loth to give up their Sunday markets, for Sunday was a day when people, free of weekday duties and congregated for church, would be most likely to prove good customers. With markets one usually associates fairs which, like them, were held on licence from the king, but which were less freely given. The king would sell the privilege or grant it to a favourite abbey. It was to churches that the most famous fairs belonged, among them Winchester. Bishop Walkelin of Winchester obtained the grant of a three-day fair from William II. It was so successful that it provided funds for completing his new cathedral and convent. During the three days all trading in Winchester and for miles around (at one stage including Southampton) was forbidden except at the fair. Later it was extended to 14 and then to 24 days, and it became a meeting-place for merchants from all over Europe. Merrymaking there was, but the great business of the fairs was buying and selling. The greater ones were centres of international trade and places where the members of the royal court replenished their wardrobes. There they bought the innumerable pelts which lined their robes and so made life possible in an English winter, at a time when central heating meant a wood fire in the middle of a large and draughty hall.

Excavations are going on in Winchester to establish, among other things, the layout of the Norman town, but, however successful these excavations may be, they cannot reproduce the visual image of houses which exist now only as a few relics of foundations. There are, however, still standing a few stone houses, which have survived the ravages of time and the urge to

77

Jew's House, Lincoln, mid-twelfth century

build bigger and better. Two of the most famous are in Lincoln on Steep Hill, itself a narrow, medieval-type street, usable only by pedestrian traffic. One of the two houses is traditionally known as the Jew's House. The second, in the same street, may have been a twelfth-century Jewish synagogue. The Jew's House has not passed unscathed through eight centuries, but enough of the original remains to show that it had a centre doorway opening into a passage from front to back, and a first-floor room. This was the solar with two windows, each of two lights, and a wall chimney, which was over the front door. If this is taken to represent the town house of a well-to-do citizen, whether Jewish or not, in the twelfth century, in what was then a flourishing city, it is clear that for the less prosperous the standard of comfort would be lower.

In all that has been said of towns, nothing has so far been said of London, which so excelled the rest as to be in a category of its own. The area of the city proper was comprised between the Tower of London on the east and a line linking Newgate and the outlet of the River Fleet on the west, just to the west of St Paul's. Smithfield and the great Priory of St Bartholomew were outside the walls on the north, Yet within this small area there lived a population of well over 10,000, probably more than twice the size of that of any other town in England. Although London is not described in Domesday Book, we have many sources of information for the period and among them the famous description by Fitz-Stephen, probably written about 1180. FitzStephen was writing the life of the martyr, St Thomas Becket, a Londoner like himself.

We learn that London and its suburbs had 13 great conventual churches and 126 parish churches, that it had three great schools, St Paul's, St Martin-le-Grand and Holy Trinity, and that others could be licensed, that on holy days the masters assembled their pupils at the church whose feast day it was and that there they disputed with each other in logic and rhetoric and competed in verse and grammar. One gathers that the meetings were not characterised by decorum, for the boys hurled abuse and gibes at each other. There were three castles, the royal castle in the east—the White Tower—and two castles in the west—Baynard's Castle and Montfichet Tower. Whereas the Anglo-Saxon custom of nobles and thegns having houses in their local towns had tended to die out after the Conquest, yet London was again an exception for, says FitzStephen, 'almost all Bishops, Abbots and Magnates of England are, as it were, citizens and freemen of the City of London, having lordly habitations there, whither they repair and wherein they make lavish display when called by our lord the King . . . to Councils and great assemblies or drawn thither by their own affairs'. Not only could the barons be considered as citizens of London, but the citizens themselves were the King's barons of his city of London and as such they are referred to in the Great Charter, 1215.

Medieval seal of the Barons of London

Those bishops and abbots and barons who had houses in London often had them in the vicinity of their gates of entrance. They were not congregated together in one quarter of the city— the West End. Between the huddled shops and houses of London's citizens would appear a wide gateway, giving on to a paved courtyard, with

hall and chamber, kitchens and garden and, in the case of
a great churchman, a separate chapel—a bit of country spacious-
ness in a crowded city. But was it so crowded? The narrow
shops and house fronts would suggest that it was, but there
was often a considerable extension to the rear, permitting
outhouses and possibly a garden, where its owner could
walk or sit. FitzStephen boasts that London had conduits
and sewers. These last seem to have been open drains down the
centre of the generally unpaved streets, innocent of sidewalks.
There the garbage of the city would be cast, from ordinary
household refuse to the entrails of slaughtered animals. There
also the dogs and pigs would hunt for titbits. The almost entire
absence of public conveniences meant that the streets and walls
were fouled. There was a public convenience at Queenhithe, so
placed that it drained into the Thames. There were cesspits in
the gardens of most houses. If they were walled they need be no
further than two-and-a-half feet from the party boundary; if
unwalled they must be five feet. ' Gong' was the old English
word for latrine and gong fermor the man whose profession it was
periodically to clear the refuse. His pay, surely well earned, was
about three times that of an ordinary unskilled worker. It is
reported of one of these twelfth-century sanitation experts that he
just could not stand the smell of a snuffed candle! Of the conduits
mentioned by FitzStephen it is difficult to find trace. The first
definite reference is to 1237, when Gilbert de Sandford granted
to the City of London all the springs and waters in his fief of
Tyburn, with the right to bring them by conduit through his
land and to have access to his land for the repair of pipes, towers
and reservoirs. In the twelfth century the water cart must
have been the answer to the water problem.

Clocks were not unknown at this time, but they were water
clocks and possessed only by the great. London took its time
from St Martin le Grand, which pealed the canonical hours,
peals which were taken up by the other churches. Work started
at dawn and went on till sunset, a long working day in summer
and a short one in winter, when in many trades the wages were
lower. The worker made up for his long hours by the number of
holy days, of which there were several in each month. But if he

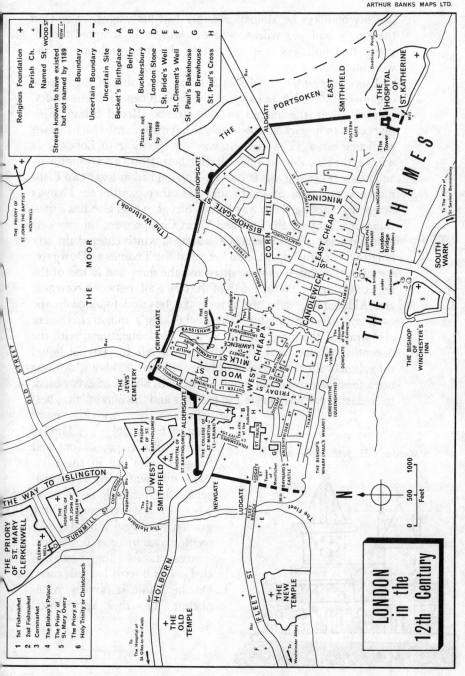

LONDON in the 12th Century

Religious Foundation +
Parish Ch. +
Named St. — WOOD ST
Streets known to have existed but not named by 1189 — BOW L^e
Boundary - - - -
Uncertain Boundary - · - ·
Uncertain Site ?
Becket's Birthplace A
Belfry B
Bucklersbury C
London Stone D
St. Bride's Well E
St. Clement's Well F
Places not named by 1189 { St. Paul's Bakehouse and Brewhouse G
St. Paul's Cross H

1 1st Fishmarket
2 2nd Fishmarket
3 Cornmarket
4 The Bishop's Palace
5 The Priory of St. Mary Overy
6 The Priory of Holy Trinity or Christchurch

(N.B. The width of streets has not been drawn to scale.)

had his holidays he almost certainly lost his wages, except on the king's building works, where it was early accepted that of every two holidays one counted to the king and one to the workman.

There were many crafts in London and some of them were organised into gilds as early as the twelfth century. The crafts, judging from the names of the streets—Bread Street, Fish market, Candlewick Street—seem to have frequented each its own particular area. The custom was not peculiar to London, as witness the Shambles at York, the Butchers' Rows in various towns and other revealing street names. London had at least two Fish-markets, one near St Paul's and the other parallel to Thames Street and linking them was Friday Street, which also has something of a fishy smell. East and West Cheaps were the markets east and west of the Walbrook, a stream which entered the city north-west of Bishopsgate and entered the Thames at Dowgate, between the vintry or wine quay and the quay and house of the men of Cologne. To the north of the city wall, between Newgate and Aldersgate, were the priory and hospital founded in the early twelfth century by Rahere, the king's minstrel. Rahere also drained the marsh to the west of his foundations, with the exception of one pool, the Horse Pool, left to provide liquid refreshment for the horses. For here, on every Friday which was not a feast day, was held a horse fair, with horses of every kind, from destriers (war horses) to palfreys and the horses 'that best befit esquires, moving more roughly but nimbly .... Thither come all the Earls, Barons and Knights, who are in the City, and with them many of the citizens, whether to look on or to buy.' In another part of the ground were agricultural implements and animals, ploughs and 'mares fit for the ploughs', sledges and two-horsed carts. On the whole it is very reminiscent of the agricultural

Matilda's Hospital in London

82

shows held all over the country in the summer in our own day.

The southern boundary of the city was the Thames, with Thames Street linking up the various quays and docks, like Queenhithe with its watergate and the ocean-going ships in its basin. To the west of Botolf's Wharf was the great London Bridge linking the city with Southwark on the south bank, and just to the west of the wooden bridge in FitzStephen's day were the foundations of a new stone bridge, begun in 1176 but not finished until 1209. Also on the river bank, and singled out by FitzStephen as something very special and worthy of note, was a cookshop,

The great bell which summoned the borough court, or portman-moot, of London

certainly a very special kind of cookshop in that it catered for all classes of the community. If a citizen had unexpected guests there was no need for his wife to worry, he could take them to the cookshop, where, according to the seasons, he could get 'viands, dishes roast, fried and boiled, fish great and small, the coarser flesh for the poor, the more delicate for the rich, such as venison and birds, both big and little', and remember that the vintry was but a step away!

London, like other boroughs, had its borough court, its portmanmoot, which met three times a year in the open space near St Paul's. No special summons was issued. The citizens gathered at the ringing of the great bell of St Paul's. This borough court was the equivalent of the shire court and the 'Greater London' of the twelfth century included the small county of Middlesex. But London could not be governed in so primitive a fashion. It had had other courts even before 1066. It was divided into wards, probably 24, each with its own regional court—the equivalent of a hundred court—under the presidency of its alderman. The main day-to-day business of the city was carried on in the Husting, which met every Monday in the Guildhall. It sat around on four benches and dealt with matters concerning foreign merchants, weights and measures, and the like.

London life, as compared with life in provincial towns, had probably the same attraction as it has today. One thing which tended to give London its special character and importance was the presence, two miles upriver from its western boundary, of the great Abbey of Westminster and the adjoining royal palace, which became more and more the headquarters of government. The great tower of the palace was visible from the outskirts of London. The fact that the king, in a wandering life, probably spent more time in his Westminster palace than in any other meant that his courtiers and visiting magnates needed accommodation. The two miles between Westminster and London constituted a flourishing and aristocratic suburb, with the great house of the Bishop of Lincoln and the castle of the Order of the Knights Templar, surrounded by an ugly growth of timber buildings, among the most outstanding. These houses had more room for expansion than those in the city, and orchards and gardens were very much in evidence.

In Roman times most roads had radiated from London. The same phenomenon was present in the fourteenth century and it was probably true also of the eleventh and twelfth, although our evidence for this particular period is confined to suggestive place names like Londonstrete. These roads radiating from London, and therefore converging on London, must have been among the busiest in the country with a constant coming and going of parties on horseback, mule or foot, with waggons for heavy transport; parties, because it was more congenial to travel in groups and also safer, in that the roads round London ran through wooded country and the woods

Travellers

84

often grew right to the edge of the road, giving shelter to robbers and other undesirable characters. The old Anglo-Saxon law that woods and undergrowth should be cleared to a depth of ten feet from main roads was probably never well enforced and seems to have been a dead letter in the Norman period.

This forest country round London was good hunting country. Says FitzStephen:

> Hard by there stretches a great forest with wooded glades and lairs of wild beasts, deer both red and fallow, wild boars and bulls .... many of the citizens delight in taking their sport with birds of the air, merlins and falcons and the like and with dogs that wage warfare in the woods, The citizens have the special privilege of hunting in Middlesex, Hertfordshire and all Chiltern, and in Kent as far as the River Cray.

Privilege indeed, when the kings recognised in the citizens of their greatest city rights which they denied to many of their greatest barons!

Further Reading

J. Tait, *The Medieval English Borough*, 1936
C. Stephenson, *Borough and Town*
F. M. Stenton, *Norman London* (Historical Association Pamphlet, 93–4), 1934
M. D. Lobel, *The Borough of Bury St Edmunds*
F. W. F. Hill, *Medieval Lincoln*, 1948
G. T. Salusbury, *Street Life in Medieval England* (2nd ed.), 1948

V

The Church

We are looking at this period from the mid-1960s, with a Vatican Council struggling with the question of Christian tolerance and even Christian unity, and with other churches, especially in England, working towards Church unity in face of the scepticism or active hostility of a large section of the population, and of the anti-clericalism and anti-religion of the governments of the communist world. What do we see nine centuries back? We see a Europe in which, except for certain Moslem areas in Spain and South Italy and a fringe of paganism in northern Scandinavia, the Christian Church, with centres at Rome and Constantinople, is indeed an 'established' Church. Any overt departure from its tenets is heresy and liable to condign punishment.

One obvious deduction follows from this. The Church, as the Church of Everyman, played a much more important part in the life of the nation than it does today. It was the backcloth against which life was lived and it is only through a realisation of the magnitude of the Church's part that we can really come to an understanding of the lives of those who were technically laymen. Also important is the proportion of the whole population which found itself, in some form or other, enlisted in the ranks of churchmen. It was incredibly high and it must have affected almost every family in the land. There were two main branches of churchmen. In the first place there were the 'religious', that is the men and women who had officially withdrawn from the world to live in monasteries and nunneries. In the second there were the secular clergy, from archbishops to deacons, whose task it was to bring religion to the laity.

Monasticism had had a great revival in England in the tenth century under three great leaders, Duncan, Ethelwold and Oswald, but by 1066 much of the force of the revival had spent itself. There still survived from the period of monastic fervour monk-bishops, who were both bishops of their dioceses and abbots of monasteries, which had replaced the usual cathedral chapters. Winchester and Worcester were the two most important of these in 1066. Including the cathedral monasteries, there were 35 houses of monks and six of nuns on the eve of the Conquest. They were not large. Excluding the cathedral monasteries, only four had more than 40 monks and 13 had six or less, but between them they seem to have accounted for about one-sixth of the wealth of England south of the Tees. Meanwhile on the Continent in the eleventh century, more particularly from mid-century, there was a great revival of religious life, which showed itself in the reform of the Papacy, in renewed enthusiasm for monastic life (especially for the reformed monasteries which had sprung from Cluny in the early tenth century) and, towards the end of the eleventh century, in a tremendous upsurge of religious feeling, which could not be contained by the humdrum religious activities of daily life, nor by the very worthy and respectable Benedictine monasticism, whether represented by monasteries of the old type or by the newer Cluniac houses. This religious enthusiasm led, among the warlike elements of the population, to the First Crusade, preached by Pope Urban II in 1095, and, among the more reflective types to a breakaway from the old comfortable monastic life towards more ascetic ideals. This brought about the foundation, in the late eleventh century, of the Cistercian, Carthusian and other orders and, in the early twelfth century, of more orders, particularly of canons, who were secular clergy living a communal life. In Normandy, in the decades before the English adventure, there was much enthusiasm for monastic life. Dukes and barons alike founded monasteries or endowed existing ones, and reforming abbots, either trained at Cluny or influenced by Cluny, led the way.

When William came to England he had several reasons for being interested in the English ecclesiastical scene. He had fought and won under a consecrated banner sent him by the

STIGANT
ARCHI—EPS

*The Anglo-Saxon Archbishop Stigand
who was deposed in 1070*

Pope. His invasion had been in the nature of a crusade: therefore he was committed to reforming the English Church, a commitment which suited his own inclinations. The English Archbishop of Canterbury, Stigand, had been uncanonically appointed and he also held a number of sees and church preferments. As soon as he was deposed by a Papal Legate in 1070, William brought over to England as Archbishop of Canterbury an Italian, Lanfranc, who had been Prior of the little monastery of Le Bec and then Abbot of William's own foundation of St Stephen's, Caen. William as king and Lanfranc as a monk were vitally concerned with the English monasteries, comparatively few and small, but very rich, not by any means all of them very strict in the observance of their rule and most of them tending to be strongholds of English nationalism. William was also determined to incorporate the monasteries (and the cathedrals) in his feudal plans for military service.

Not many abbots were deposed but those that were, and others who succumbed to natural causes, were replaced by French, mostly Norman monks. On the whole they were very fine men, great reformers and excellent administrators, but, except where colonies of monks were also brought to England, the new abbot must often have felt isolated in an alien and hostile community. However, these foreign abbots seem, either among their compatriots or among the subject English, to have found recruits. The existing monasteries grew. Christchurch under Lanfranc achieved its century and Gloucester under Abbot Serlo increased from ten to 100 in 32 years (1072–1104). The nunneries also grew, becoming in many cases havens of refuge for the womenfolk of dispossessed English landowners. The Normans also founded new monasteries: one's own monastic foundation became a prestige symbol. William himself founded and endowed the great Abbey of Battle in memory of his victory, though it took long in the building and was only consecrated under his successor.

The monastic way of life was founded on the Rule of St Benedict, which was interpreted by each monastery in its own way, but the rules laid down by Lanfranc for his cathedral monastery of Christchurch, Canterbury, were probably fairly widely adopted and give us a picture of the monk's life in the late eleventh century. In the first place, how did one become a monk? The Venerable Bede in the seventh century was offered as a child to the monastery of Jarrow. This seems to have been a usual method of recruitment of the black monks (Benedictine and Cluniac) until the middle of the twelfth century. The choice was made not by the monk-to-be but by his parents, who might be influenced by religious or by economic considerations. There was a tendency, even before the Conquest, for landowners to leave their property to one son, so preserving its unity. This hardened into a rule in the Norman period. The monastic life would provide at least one of the younger sons with an assured future among men who, for the most part, would be his social equals. One well-known oblate was Orderic Vitalis, the historian of the Norman Conquest. Son of a Norman father and English mother, he was born near Shrewsbury shortly after the Conquest. At the age of ten he was handed over by his father to a monk, Rainald, to be offered to a Norman monastery, St Evroul, where, when he was 11, he was clothed and tonsured. Most of these children seem to have accepted their fate philosophically—a reflection of the part played by the Church in the lives of

Twelfth-century picture of the tonsuring of St Guthlac

89

everyone. There must, however, have been some among them
who felt no vocation, were irked by the limitations on their
freedom, or bored by the monotony of the life. Misfits such as
these may have been responsible for some of the laxity and for
some of the scandals of which we have record.

Lanfranc legislated for these 'children of the cloister'. They
were in the overall care of a child master, responsible for their
education and training. They were tonsured like the monks. They
shared the same dormitory. They must never be alone together
nor speak together. They shared the service of the church and
were invaluable in the choir singing. Slight allowance only was
made for their tender years. They were excused the first service,
at about 2 a.m., and they seem to have been allowed breakfast
during the monks' chapter. The children had their own chapter,
a replica of that of the monks. The Abingdon Chronicle relates a
story of Queen Edith, wife of the Confessor, visiting the monastery while the children were at breakfast—of dry bread. She
made a gift of property to the monastery, earmarked for the provision of morning milk for the children. Before we expend our
pity on these infants, deprived of home life and comforts and
of the freedom and irresponsibility of childhood, we must
remind ourselves that it was not from indulgent homes in
an affluent society that the children were exiled, and that
the comparatively high standard of skill and care in the
monastic infirmary must have given them a better chance to
survive the ills of childhood
than had their secular brothers.
But one of the last recorded
cases of oblation was about 1150
and in 1216 the practice became
illegal. It was killed by criticism
from the new orders, which accepted only adults making their
choice freely, and probably also
by the opening up of more
careers for younger sons in the
expanding organisation of the
twelfth century. Children were

Monks' procession into Church

90

still sent to monastic schools, but without the obligation to become monks.

The Rule envisaged a minutely organised life for every member of the community, but in the early twelfth century the Abbot withdrew to his own 'lodging', surrounded by his own officials and servants. More and more of the monks became officials of the monastery, priors and sub-priors, the sacrist in charge of the altar services and the fabric, the cellarer in charge of the stores, the chamberlain responsible for the monks' clothing, bedding, baths, etc., the infirmarian in charge of the infirmary and many others. Each of these offices could be subdivided, but the actual physical work, for instance the cooking, was done by hired servants. As these officers were occupied many hours a day on the business of the monastery

Adam, Sacrist of St Alban's in the late twelfth century

and its estates, the full timetable was kept only by the simple monks, novices and children.

For the purpose of the monastic timetable the year was divided into three, Winter (from 13 September to Ash Wednesday), Lent and Summer. Probably the most noticeable difference to us would be the mealtimes, in winter and Lent one meal a day, taken in winter at 2 p.m. and in Lent about 6 p.m. In summer there were two meals, at midday and 6 p.m., with a siesta after the midday meal. An evening drink was allowed in winter, at first water, then beer and on certain occasions wine or wine and cake.

The monks retired to their dormitory at 7 p.m. to beds filled with straw, which was changed annually. They slept in their habits, clad in night shoes, ready to file down into the church for the first service of the day, at about 2 a.m. We have to remind ourselves that the church was unheated! The day was then divided into various services, with, at 8 a.m., a break for changing into day shoes, washing in the lavatorium and

combing hair and beards. Soon after 9 would be the daily chapter and this would be followed by a period of work in the cloister. For those who had the ability, this would consist in writing, copying or illuminating books, and the twelfth century has left us some very fine specimens of illumination. The place set apart for this work was the north walk of the cloister, sheltered by the nave of the church, against which it was set, and open to any rays of winter sunshine. Even so the task of the artist or writer must at times have been painful and we learn from Orderic Vitalis that there were days on which he simply could not write his beloved history. The work period lasted for about two-and-a-half hours and the silence rule was relaxed to allow for necessary talk about work. After further services the monks had what was literally a breakfast, at about 2 p.m. According to the Rule this was the only meal in winter, but different houses varied their custom. Lanfranc allowed two meals on feast days throughout the winter. At Peterborough a century later two meals were allowed until 1 October, during St Martin's week, from Christmas to Epiphany, and on all Sundays. After the meal there was a period of private prayer or reading and then the Maundy

Late eleventh-century copy of the Commentary on St Augustine written for the Bishop of Durham, William of St Calais, who is pictured with the illuminator, Robert Benjamin, at his feet

ceremony of washing the feet of 12 poor men in the cloister. Certain abbots, including Abbot Walter de Lucy of Battle, brother of Henry II's Justiciar, performed this washing in person, and Abbot Walter did not shun even the lepers. After further services the monks retired to their beds. The long day was over.

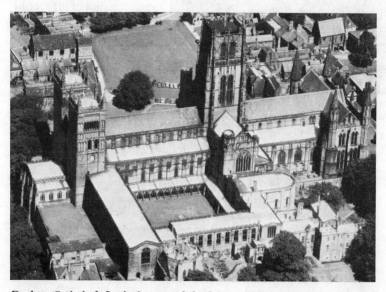

Durham Cathedral. In the foreground the cloisters, showing the shelter afforded by the nave. The original scriptorium would be the sheltered cloister, open to the midday sun

It may be said that the *nutriti*—those who had been tonsured in childhood—were inured to the regular monotonous life, and that those who entered later in life had deliberately chosen it. In spite of this, the lack of variety, of the unexpected, in the life of the cloister did cause trouble. The monastic officials had an avenue of escape. The full routine was maintained only by the simple choir monks and some of them tried to relieve the monotony by undertaking copying for outsiders. The monks had a Latin name for this boredom, *accidia*, and a recognised treatment:

93

Monks (two of whom are priests)

the patient was made to sit on a special stone in the chapter house, but we are not told how effective the cure was.

St Benedict had planned both the routine and the diet of his monks with the climate and vegetation of central Italy in mind. The monks were not to eat the flesh of quadrupeds, which might be considered to include all meat, but in England was often interpreted as not including the flesh of birds. With this doubtful exception, the monastic menu had to consist of fish, eggs, vegetables and bread. In the deterioration of monastic life, which was characteristic of many monasteries in the last decades of the old English state, one of the first relaxations was probably that of diet. Many of the monasteries were rich and if meat were available they could get it. We know from the annals of Winchester that the first Norman Prior of the Old Minster, Simeon, found the monks eating meat. With considerable tact, he substituted for the meat dishes such exquisitely prepared fish dishes that there was no grumbling at the change. If Gerald of Wales, who was no friend of the monks, is to be believed, the pleasures of the table had not lost their attraction almost a century later. He tells how

> the monks of St Swithin's, Winchester, together with their Prior, prostrated themselves in the mud before Henry II and complained to him with tears and lamentations that Bishop Richard, whom they had as their head in lieu of an abbot, had deprived them of three dishes. And when the king enquired how many dishes were left them, they replied 'Ten'. 'And I', said the King, 'am content in my Court with three. Perish your bishop, if he does not reduce your dishes to the number of mine!'

The normal diet was adequate—a pound of bread per person, with cheese and vegetables and two dishes made from cereals, beans or eggs. The second meal in summer would consist of part of the pound of bread with fruit and vegetables. But the custom grew up of supplementing this diet with pittances, the province of an officer specially created—the pittancer. The idea was that there could be extra dishes of fish and eggs on feast days. There might be as many as three or four pittances a meal, each consisting of an extra dish between every two monks, for the medieval habit was for two diners to eat from one dish, using fingers, of course! In Saxon times the drink was probably beer, with mead or very occasionally wine on special feast days. The Normans brought with them wine-drinking habits and they even managed to grow the vine in the South and South-East and in the Severn valley.

Some relaxation of the Rule, even in respect of eating meat, was allowed to the sick, and the rule of silence was gradually waived for those who had undergone the favourite medieval cure of blood-letting. This, towards the end of the twelfth century, became a routine affair, but even before this it had become customary for the monastery to set aside two rooms for limited conversation, one for the abbot and guests, the other for officials and private monks. These were called *locutoria* or parlours.

The black monks were not cut off from mankind. It was one of their functions to succour the poor and afflicted and many monasteries actually maintained a number of poor pensioners. Before the Conquest they were the abbot's responsibility. After the Conquest a new officer appeared, the almoner, and before long we have the almonry within the monastic precincts. Funds, even manors, were set aside to provide for this work of charity and the almoner, with a staff of servants, could also expect a proportion of the bread issuing from the monastic bakehouse and of the vegetables from the garden. In addition the monasteries were expected to welcome travellers, rich or poor. In the case of the poor, such hospitality filled a great need. Pilgrimages to churches, which had some particularly venerated relic, brought crowds to the monasteries and complicated the monastic house-

Christ and two disciples dressed as twelfth-century pilgrims

keeping, but their offerings contributed appreciably to the revenues and especially to building funds.

The black monk houses made their impact on society in many other ways, of which two may be instanced here. They were landlords on a very large scale, having in their possession many manors. They controlled in the twelfth century 20 boroughs, which were wholly on monastic estates. In the case of Bury St Edmunds, the sacrist acted on behalf of the convent, collecting rents, tolls and other dues. The monastic landlords were, in general, more conservative than secular ones and were loth to give charters of privilege which would limit their control or in any way lessen their profit. In the second place the monasteries and other religious communities, such as canons, owned about a quarter of the parish churches in England. Many of these churches were built by landowners who could give or sell them as they pleased, and monasteries were favoured recipients of such gifts. The monks themselves could not serve as parish priests, so they either appointed someone to do the job at the lowest salary he would accept, while they collected the tithe, or they farmed out the tithe to a layman for a fixed sum and he provided the priest, taking care to ensure his middleman's profit.

Until 1128 the only monasteries in England were those of the black monks, but in that year the first Cistercian house was founded at Waverley in Surrey and was quickly followed by Tintern (1131), Rievaulx and Fountains (1132). By 1216 there were 68 Cistercian houses in England and Wales and the number would undoubtedly have been higher, but for the fact that the General Council of Cîteaux, the governing body of the whole order, legislated against new foundations. The houses of white monks, as they were called from their tunics of undyed wool, were on the whole larger than those of the black monks, and they contained not only the full monks but lay brothers, the numerous would-be monks whose illiteracy made them unable to take part in the services of the church. These were a very important element in the community life, for by their Rule, given them in 1119 by their English Abbot, Stephen Harding, the Cistercians were not allowed to hire labour, nor were they allowed to hold manors and receive services therefrom in lieu of rent. They were to avoid the snares into which the Benedictines had fallen by keeping clear of all feudal entanglements. In their churches and other buildings they were to eschew all magnificence, from towers to embroidered copes and jewelled altar vessels. The same applied to their persons. They were allowed no fur-lined garments and no linen next the skin, just two tunics of undyed wool. They were not even allowed breeches, the universal garment for the male, except on journeys. This provided fuel for the malicious wit of Walter Map, who hated the Cistercians. He tells the story of how, when travelling in the train of Henry II, his party met a Cistercian, who, recognising the king, turned to make obeisance, when an unkind wind lifted his tunics and exposed the nakedness beneath to the ribald laughter of the courtiers. It was Walter Map who declared that, when he swore as a judge to do justice to all, he added a clause excluding Jews and Cistercians. When his friend Gerald of Wales told him of two Cistercians who had become Jews, he retorted that, having decided to change their lives for the better, they should have made their conversion complete by becoming Christians!

Cistercian monk

Gerald's *bêtes noires* were the black monks, but he had little love for the Cistercians either. It was bound to happen that in the course of time some benefactor should give the Cistercians land which included manors and churches. According to their rule they should have refused it. 'Not a bit of it,' says Gerald, 'they drove away the inhabitants and closed the churches in order both to keep their Rule and to keep their land.' There is no doubt, however, that the Cistercians had a higher reputation for adherence to their Rule and for austerity than had the older foundations and that they attracted both more recruits and more benefactions. At the beginning, most of these were in wild places, far from the habitations of men, like the Yorkshire moors and the wilder parts of Wales. The fact that the Cistercians had to clothe as well as feed themselves turned them willynilly into sheep farmers—and to good purpose, in that they produced such excellent sheep and in such great numbers that their wool was more than sufficient for their needs. This was ultimately to prove their undoing. In an age which saw a great expansion of the cloth industry and the wool trade, they had wool to sell. They entered commerce and in many cases it became more important to them than the soul's welfare. The beginning of the decline was visible before the end of the twelfth century.

Fountains Abbey, Yorkshire: the twelfth-century cellarium

This same century, which saw the appeal of the communal religious life so intensified for men, witnessed a similar phenomenon in the case of their sisters. Women also wanted to withdraw from the world. Some followed the Cistercian Rule and many, in eastern England, the English foundation of Gilbert of Sempringham, whose houses probably enclosed several thousand women by the end of the century. There were full nuns, whose knowledge of ecclesiastical Latin was at least as good as that of their brothers in religion, and lay sisters, often from peasant or artisan homes, to whose lot fell the menial tasks. Most of the nunneries seem to have been much poorer than the houses for men and at times the nuns were short of the bare necessities of life.

There were, however, men and women who deliberately chose to be short of these bare necessities, those to whom the monastic life was not sufficiently a life of deprivation and who sought not an ordered routine but an undisciplined asceticism. These were the hermits and hermitesses, anchorites and anchoresses, who built themselves huts either in the wilds or near some church or monastery, which could minister to their spiritual needs. Such a one was Christina of Markyate, the daughter of a comparatively wealthy landowner in the diocese of Lincoln. As a girl she vowed herself to celibacy and, after a long fight with her family and the suitor to whom her father had betrothed her, she was eventually allowed to live her own life in a cell not far from the Abbey of St Albans. She achieved considerable local fame, was a spiritual adviser of Abbot Geoffrey of St Albans and through him even sent a present of embroidered slippers to the Pope. It was to another woman recluse that the Cistercian, St Ailred of Rievaulx, about the middle of the twelfth century, wrote his guide to a hermitess's life. He wrote in Latin, so she must have been an educated woman. She is not to starve, but must never satisfy her hunger and she must avoid any delicate foods. Her diet is to consist of a little vegetable and meal mixed with fat or milk or pease on retiring. Her clothes are to be coarse, in summer a tunic and two stuff chemises and in winter a sheepskin, hose and shoes and a black veil for her head. She may keep herself by her handiwork, but should not run a girls' school, although she may teach girls, if it will save them from being taught with boys! On the whole except for the teaching, a life not unlike that of the peasant woman, but with less work.

All told there must have been a few thousand women and many thousand men officially withdrawn from the world. To these must be added the mighty forces of the secular clergy. In this matter of priesthood, the period we are dealing with saw a great change. The least noticeable change would be in the parish clergy. Before the Conquest many of them were appointed by the landlords and their most important function was to act as chaplains to their patrons, and this state of affairs was to continue. For the rest they were very much part and parcel of village life, sharing in the agricultural routine and distinguished mainly by a sketchy knowledge of church Latin and a limited ability to read it. Most of them would be married and a parson would often be followed in the parish by his son. The eleventh and twelfth centuries saw an attempt to enforce celibacy on the clergy. Lanfranc of Canterbury was a realist. He did not attempt to make priests give up their wives, but he decreed that in future no priest was to marry and that, if a married man wished to enter the priesthood, he must first separate from his wife. At the end of our period the problem was still unsolved. The priest's hearthwoman (*focaria*) was now called his concubine and her offspring declared illegitimate, but she was still there.

In 1066 nine of the 16 bishops in England were monks, the abbots of monasteries which had taken over the functions of the cathedral chapters. Edward the Confessor had found this state of affairs on his accession and he had accepted it. He had, however, brought with him from Normandy the custom of having a court chapel, staffed with clerks who could help him in the administrative work of government, in fact an embryo civil service. From time to time he appointed one of his chapel priests to a bishopric. It rewarded the priest without depriving the king of his services, for the bishops were very much a part of the administration. The position of the Royal Chapel was enhanced when William became king and it never looked back. Royal clerks took more and more share in government. Under

Henry I they dominated the newly developed Exchequer. The Chancellor and Treasurer and most of the royal judges were priests and they all looked to a bishopric as their ultimate reward. There was an ever increasing demand for clerks to staff the developing Civil Service.

Demand creates supply. Many young men from the rising classes in towns went to school. They became clerks, if only in minor orders, because it was inconceivable that anyone other than a clerk should be interested in, or should receive, education. 'Lay' was synonymous with 'illiterate'. So the numbers of secular clerks grew until they exceeded those of the religious. Quite a small proportion of them would expect to get cure of souls, and to sons of priests there was the bar of illegitimacy. So the ranks of the clergy were swollen by those seeking jobs which would nowadays go to laymen. Not all of them found employment.

Archbishop in full canonicals

It was almost certainly from the ranks of the unbeneficed, and also unemployed, clergy that the clerical criminals of Henry II's reign were recruited. 'X, of no fixed address', who figures so largely in the crime columns of our newspapers today, would have had his twelfth-century counterpart in 'X, clerk, of no fixed address'. To him and to his kind could be attributed many of the murders, rapes and other crimes, which were such a headache to Henry II—and he had one headache which does not afflict the modern state. His officers could not try or punish an offending clerk. Once arrested he could claim 'benefit of clergy' and, if the claim was attested by the bishop, he must be handed over to the bishop's court, where the heaviest penalty was deprivation of his clerical status. It was this state of affairs which helped to precipitate the crisis between Henry II and his one-time friend,

101

Archbishop Thomas Becket, the culmination of which—the murder of Becket in Canterbury Cathedral in 1170—is probably the most publicised event of the twelfth century.

If there were archdeacons before the Conquest they were very few in number. The office really developed in the Norman period. As his name implies, the archdeacon was not, or was only rarely, in priest's orders. There were usually three or four to a diocese and it was their job to supervise and discipline the parish priests. On the whole they were a worldly lot. We have already met two, Gerald of Wales, Archdeacon of St David's, and Walter Map, Archdeacon of Oxford. Gerald probably spent rather more of his time in his diocese than did Walter, who seems to have been primarily a courtier. Gerald gives us some idea of the wardrobe of an archdeacon. He was sitting in his chamber pursuing his studies when he heard an uproar outside. It was the poor and needy crying for alms.

> And straightway he was filled with pity for them and looking at his cloaks and hoods and the pellices of foreign furs [squirrel, marten, etc] and conies, all hung upon poles, he ordered that whatever there was among them of vair or miniver and cony should be sold and the money distributed for the benefit of the poor. This was done forthwith and from that hour the Archdeacon was content with cloaks of lambskin.

Murder of Thomas Becket, Archbishop of Canterbury

The bishops and the greater abbots, at least the more worldly among them, lived as did the greater barons. Their households were much the same. Canon Law did try to put some limit on the bishop's train. He was allowed to travel with 30 horses and all that that implied in servants and followers, and, in spite of Canon Law, he was more often than not also accompanied by dogs and hawks and their attendants. Even an archdeacon was officially allowed seven horses and, like his bishop, he usually added thereunto the agents of his sporting pastimes.

Deacon, priest and bishop

Stories reach us of episcopal gluttony. Episcopal meals equalled, if they did not excel, those of the lay baronage. The bishop had the excuse, as had the monks, that, the more there was provided for him, the more there would be for the poor. This was the case of Samson, Bishop of Worcester after the Conquest. He once sat down to a dish of 80 chickens: one hopes that the poor of Worcester fared well! Some of the bishops seem indistinguishable from barons. Odo, Bishop of Bayeux, half-brother of the Conqueror, said Grace before meat in his capacity as priest, but fought with the rest in the battle that followed, and is only distinguishable in the Tapestry by his name embroidered above him. After the Conquest he was to double his bishopric with the earldom of Kent. The Bishop of Durham was secular lord of a great area in the North-East, where he had his castles, his barons, knights and sheriffs and was responsible for the defence of the North against the Scots. His castle of Durham is now the nucleus of one of the colleges of the university. Not all bishops were of this type, so perhaps it is well to conclude with one who was outstanding among those who put their spiritual functions first—St Hugh of Avalon, Bishop of Lincoln at the end of our period.

Further Reading

D. Knowles, *The Monastic Orders in England, 943–1216*
E. Power, *Medieval English Nunneries*
M. Deanesley, *Sidelights on the Anglo-Saxon Church,*
————, *Chronicle of Brakelonde* (Nelson Medieval Texts)

Bishop Odo of Bayeux in Battle

VI

Learning and Literature

Pre-Conquest England had its schools but unfortunately we know little enough about them. There were monastic schools, mainly for the children of the cloister, but probably catering for a few others. However, the education was primarily a preparation for the monastic life. There must have been schools attached to the greater churches, especially when polyphonic singing was introduced. The education in these schools would vary, some teaching the elements of reading, others ensuring merely that the choristers knew their texts by heart. There must have been other schools. London had at least three after the Conquest and it is most unlikely that they were all new creations. St Peter's, York, was founded in the eighth century and its most famous master was Alcuin, who was invited by Charlemagne to help revive education in his empire. After the eighth century the school disappears. It may or may not have survived the Danish invasions, but one of the first appointments made by the first Norman Archbishop of York was that of a schoolmaster. It seems unlikely that this was for a school which had been dead for at least two centuries.

In pre-Conquest Normandy education, as in England, was very much in the hands of the monks, but there were schools attached to cathedrals as well. Even a worldly prelate like Odo, Bishop of Bayeux, obviously had a school for, at his own expense, he sent some of the brighter boys for further education to the famous school at Liège. Two of these followed him to England, two brothers, Samson who became Bishop of Worcester and

Thomas, the first Norman Archbishop of York, the one who appointed the schoolmaster. His nephew, Samson's son, was educated in York, presumably at this same school, and later became Archbishop Thomas II of York. St Peter's maintained its position during the century. A subsequent Archbishop, Roger, secured it an endowment of 100s. a year—a sizeable sum for the period. There must have been a school at Norham-on-Tweed, for Reginald of Durham tells a story of a schoolboy culprit there, who, anticipating a hiding, took the key of the church and threw it in the river. The school was apparently held in the church and the parson was the schoolmaster. He was directed in a vision to fish in a certain part of the stream. The salmon he caught proved to have swallowed the key. We know too that there were schools at Salisbury and Lincoln, because the bishops of these places sought the aid of Archbishop Thomas I in setting them up. Later in the century Alexander of Neckham taught at both St Albans and Dunstable, and Abbot Samson of St Edmund's bought stone houses in Bury St Edmunds and assigned them to the master of the school. In fact, Theobald of Étampes, at the beginning of the century, claimed that there were schools in every town and village. Without accepting that somewhat rash statement we may believe that in Norman England schools were available for any would-be scholars.

But what were these schools? The term 'university' was not used of educational institutions until the thirteenth century. The schools therefore might be places of primary or of advanced studies. In the feast-day competitions of the London schools the younger boys seem to have shown their prowess in grammar and the like and the older boys or young men in rhetoric and dialectic. Theobald of Étampes called himself 'Magister Oxnefordie' and claimed to have taught 60–100 students at Oxford. As he taught theology they were probably adult students. Robert Pullen also taught theology in Oxford in 1133, before he was tempted by the greater delights of a career in Paris. As the lawyer Vacarius taught Roman law in Oxford for a time, and law was definitely regarded as a subject for the mature, it looks as though Oxford was already qualifying for university status. One thing is certain, either that the schools of higher education had introductory courses, which would ground the young, often very young, men in Latin or these same young men must have come to the schools with a knowledge of Latin, for all books and all tuition were in that language. Perhaps the early career of John of Salisbury, as described by himself, could be repeated in the careers of other English boys of the time. He was born in Salisbury, sometime between 1115 and 1118, and was sent as a boy to learn his Psalter from a certain priest, who apparently had a school of sorts, for John tells us that he was interested in magic and used him and the other boys in his experiments. John did not approve and apparently made very intractable material. He then left this master and he does not tell us where or how he continued his education until shortly after the death of Henry I, when he set off to the schools of Paris—for throughout the twelfth century the brightest of England's scholars were students or teachers in the schools of France. France had the most renowned teachers in the humanities and in dialectic and theology, while Italy was pre-eminent in law. An English youth, who nowadays would expect to go to Oxford or Cambridge, would in the twelfth century quite as naturally have turned to the schools of the Continent, and after 1150 it would almost certainly have been Bologna (for law) or Paris (the rest). At this time 'Paris baked the intellectual bread of Europe.'

The one-and-a-half centuries from about 1050 to 1200 is one of those exciting periods in history that we tend to label Renaissance. We have the humanist renaissance of the fifteenth and sixteenth centuries, the scientific renaissance of the seventeenth, and a technological renaissance or revolution today. The Twelfth-Century Renaissance did not revolutionise life as the technological changes of the last century have done, but it was marked by sociological change and by religious, intellectual and artistic ferment, and the Norman Conquest brought England into this 'Common Market' of the west. For centuries, since the fall of the Western Roman Empire, western Europe had been subject to constant invasion by Germanic peoples, by Saracens and by Scandinavians, and when not occupied in defence against invaders it had indulged in civil war. By the middle of the eleventh century an era of comparative stability had been achieved and men's energies could be turned into other channels than the sheer struggle for survival. In the economic sphere they turned to trade, and developing trade meant developing towns, with their busy, bustling life, so different from the stagnation of the feudal manor. In the intellectual sphere there was a deep-seated longing for knowledge. The monastic schools could not, and had no wish to, cater for this need, and intending students, drawn largely from ecclesiastical and commercial circles, flocked to the cathedral schools and other schools in cities and towns. The unenterprising would go to the local school, the more enterprising would wander off in search of the most renowned master in the subject of their choice. There was, at this time, usually one master per school and, if a great master died or was promoted to a bishopric, the school could easily lose its 'foreign' scholars and be reduced to a purely local institution. The title 'magister', denoting schoolmaster, was one to conjure with and sometime schoolmasters, who had become bishops, would still be addressed as 'master'.

In spite of what has been said above, one of the most famous schools in eleventh-century Europe was a monastic one. To the small, impoverished monastery of Le Bec in Normandy had come, in 1042, the Italian Lanfranc, a lawyer and scholar of repute, who was wandering from place to place seeking the ideal life. In Le Bec he thought he had found the peace and obscurity he wanted, but it was not to be. After about three years' anonymity, a rumour of his presence at Le Bec spread abroad and immediately students flocked there from all over Europe. The most outstanding of Lanfranc's pupils was another Italian, Anselm of Aosta, who succeeded him as schoolmaster and prior of Le Bec and later as Archbishop of Canterbury. Anselm was one of the greatest minds of the eleventh century and one of the gentlest of teachers. In fact he was the only one recorded as having no faith in the efficacy of the rod. When he left to become Archbishop in 1093 the school of Le Bec was finished, but it had already provided many of the new ecclesiastical leaders of Norman England and was, in the twelfth century, to supply another Archbishop of Canterbury, Theodore of Le Bec, whose household was a meeting place of some of the finest intellects of the time, including John of Salisbury and Thomas Becket.

For the humanities the pre-eminent school in the early twelfth century was Chartres and it owed its fame to a Breton, Bernard, usually known as Bernard of Chartres. Bernard evolved a method of teaching which was followed by his successors, his brother Thierry, William of Conches and Richard the Bishop. John of Salisbury was never a pupil of Bernard, but he was trained in the classics by William and Richard after the method of Bernard. He described this method. He says that Bernard used the classics to teach grammar and made his lessons in grammar an excuse for teaching all the subject-matter of the classics —that is the Latin classics and the little of Greek philosophy that was known in his day. The morning was spent in reading and explaining certain authors. The afternoon was devoted to grammar. The evening was spent

The rod!

in philosophical talk and religious exercises. Next morning the pupils had to produce exercises in prose or verse in imitation of the authors read the previous day. Bad work was punished by the rod. John of Salisbury tells us that the teaching of grammar was so thorough that after a year any but the most obtuse pupil could speak and write freely. It was Bernard who said, with reference to the classical authors, that the men of his time were but dwarfs, standing on the shoulders of giants, but because they so were standing they could see just that little bit farther.

Among Anselm's pupils at Le Bec had been another Anselm, probably Anselm of Lâon, who later became master of the cathedral school of that small city. Under him it became the school of schools for those interested in theology. So numerous were his would-be pupils that he could pick and choose, and those accepted were lucky if they had friends who could find them lodgings as these, in the small town, were hard to come by even at the in-

109

flated prices charged by rapacious landladies. Among other famous pupils this *doctor doctorum* taught William of Corbeil, later Archbishop of Canterbury, Alexander and Nigel, nephews of Henry's justiciar, Bishop Roger of Salisbury and later Bishops of Lincoln and Ely respectively, and Matthew, later Prior of St Martin-in-the-Fields outside London.

Another pupil of Anselm's was William of Champeaux, who subsequently took charge of the school of Notre-Dame in Paris, but he did not at this time teach theology. His subject was dialectic or, as we should call it, logic, the third of the subjects of the *Trivium* (grammar, rhetoric and dialectic), which, with the *Quadrivium* (music, arithmetic, geometry and astronomy), formed the curriculum of the schools. Dialectic, the art of argument, was probably the most popular subject in the eleventh and most of the twelfth century, and in 1100 William of Champeaux was the greatest name in dialectic: so to Paris in 1100 came Peter Abailard. This young man was the eldest son of a knight of Brittany, who took the unusual course of sending him to school. There the young Peter became so enamoured of his studies that he renounced his inheritance and a military career to follow his natural bent. This led him to various schools in the west of France and thence to Paris to study under William. The particular problem of the lectures was that of 'Universals'. Where does reality lie—in the objects we see around us and the people we are ourselves, or in Man or Animal or Tree, incorporating the generality behind the particular objects? William of Champeaux was a 'realist', holding that general ideas were real. At the opposite extreme were the 'nominalists', who thought the particular objects were real and the general ideas just *nomina* or names. These nominalists had already been in trouble with the Church, because they applied their logic to the Holy Trinity, arguing that you could not have reality in both the One and the Three, and that if you believed in the Father, Son and Holy Ghost, then they were real and the One God, comprising the Three, was but an idea, a name. It is easy to see how, in an age when religion and the Church counted for so much in men's lives, passions could be roused by such arguments and that students of all ages, from far and near, would flock to listen to the lectures of a famous master. We may be sure that there were students from England in the throng that packed the cloisters of Notre-Dame to listen to Master William, when the new student, Peter Abailard, arrived. He had already repudiated Nominalism; now he decided that the Master's Realism was nonsense, and he said so, arguing with William and drawing many students to his side. He had a chequered career, which included studying theology under Anselm at Lâon and again setting up as greater than his master and being expelled from Lâon in consequence. He made both enemies and disciples wherever he went, but he ultimately became Master at Notre-Dame and developed teaching methods which applied his skill in logic to the teaching of theology. Conceited he undoubtedly was and he must have been unbearable as a student, but as a teacher he must rank as one of the greatest of all time. The man who made Paris into a real institution, independent of any one famous master, was Peter Abailard, the scholar who took as his motto: 'By doubting we come to enquiry and by enquiring we perceive the Truth'. Question everything, take nothing on trust —a dangerous doctrine in the twelfth century! No wonder that Abailard was condemned and excommunicated. But he personi-fied the questing spirit of the century and after his death in 1142 his methods were to be accepted as orthodox and to provide the basis for teaching and writing.

During and after his time a period in the schools of Paris was a 'must' for anyone who claimed to be educated, and this applied to students from England, from Germany and from Italy. In Abailard's time there were several schools in Paris but the most im-portant were Notre-Dame on the Island and St Geneviève on the Left Bank, near what is now the Panthéon. It was here that Abailard taught when he was not al-lowed to teach at Notre-

Crossing to the schools of France

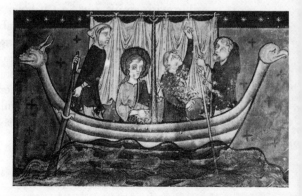

Dame and it was here that the students came in their thousands and, as the language of their lectures and their international language generally was Latin, this became known—and still is known—as the Latin Quarter. Another effect of Abailard's magnetic attraction was the proliferation of masters. No one person could teach all the crowds. Men who had followed the course set up their own lecturing stands and among them were many Englishmen, including that Robert Pullen who in 1133 had been lecturing in Oxford. John of Salisbury was never a master at Paris, but he studied there and in the vicinity for 12 years, arriving just in time to hear Master Peter before he finally gave up teaching. By this time John had quite a choice of masters and some were his own countrymen. One was Robert Pullen and another Robert of Melun, who later became Bishop of Hereford. Another English master with whom John discussed questions, though not as a pupil, was Adam du Petit Pont, so called because he held his classes there, perhaps in one of the open booths which constituted the ground floor of the little houses which lined the wooden bridge. John says of Adam: 'Would that it had pleased God that he had said well the good things that he said'. For although he believed in simple, direct speech yet in lecturing he used fanciful and involved language, because this was more likely to attract and impress pupils. In spite of this Adam must have been a dedicated teacher. When he was on a visit to his old home in Yorkshire, his family suggested that he should settle on his small patrimony, rather than scratch a scanty living in Paris. He returned to Paris, but he was ultimately tempted back to a bishopric, St Asaph's in Wales. He died probably in 1181.

To return to John of Salisbury: he spent 12 years in all, possibly with an interval in Chartres, learning thoroughly and from a number of masters all the subjects of the *Trivium* and some of the *Quadrivium*, and acquiring a supreme contempt for the new generation of students, who wanted to scamp their course in order to get on to the more profitable vocational training. Among the students who crossed the Channel were many kinds. Some had wealth and could travel and set up house with their own servants. One imagines that Gerald of Wales was among this number. Others had to work their way through: John seems to have been one of these, although he must have had enough money to see him modestly through the first few years. Then he had to take up private coaching of the sons of nobles to enable him to continue. It must have been his own experience which made him quote the 'keys of learning'

An attentive audience

(*claves discendi*) of Bernard of Chartres: 'a humble mind, a zeal for enquiry, a quiet life, silent study, poverty and a foreign land'. The last two applied to John, as they must have applied to many of his compatriots. In 1160, Henry II's Chancellor, Becket, visiting Paris on behalf of his master, received the masters and the citizens who gave hospitality to English scholars. He gave them presents from the King. A few years later the position changed. Becket, now Archbishop, quarrelled with the king and sought refuge in the dominions of Louis VII of France. Either, as some English historians say, Henry II in 1167 recalled English students from France, or, as John of Salisbury says, with war and sedition everywhere even the mildest and most civilised nation, France, was expelling her foreign students. The beneficiary of this event, whatever caused it, was Oxford. There were by this time quite a number of English schools, but Oxford was well placed, at a convenient distance from the port of Southampton and on the direct route from there to many parts of England. The school grew rapidly, until, at the end of the century it claimed to have 3,000 students, though half this number is more probable. This was in spite of the fact that, when peace was restored, Englishmen were again to be found in great numbers enrolled among the students and masters of Paris. Unless you wanted training

113

in law or medicine, Paris in the second half of the twelfth century would certainly be the school of your choice. It would be impossible to list here even those Englishmen whom we know to have studied or taught in Paris, but there is one name that we cannot omit: Stephen Langton, Cardinal of the Roman Church, Archbishop of Canterbury when our period closes and one of the leading men behind the Great Charter of 1215, first made his name as a master of the schools of Paris.

The Roman inheritance, which was almost all that was available in the west in the eleventh century, was limited in scope. The Romans were great lawyers and they had a great literature, but in philosophy and science they were no match for the Greeks they had conquered. The west, however, in the early Middle Ages lost its knowledge of Greek. Almost the last exponents of it were the Irish wandering scholars of the ninth century. Much of the Greek world was again conquered, this time in the seventh century, by the followers of Mahomet, who also conquered Persia and India. The Arabs were not great original thinkers but they absorbed the culture of their conquered peoples, the science and philosophy of ancient Greece and the mathematical knowledge of India. As, in the course of the century A.D. 630–730, the Moslems conquered North Africa and Spain, they took this composite culture with them in their wanderings. It was in the late eleventh century that the Christian west had its first contacts with this culture. Militant Christianity, spearheaded by the Normans, began the reconquest of Spain from Islam and also the island of Sicily, ruled in turn by Greeks and Moslems. In the wake of the knight went the scholar.

A twelfth-century astrolabe in use

England played her full part in this venture. The Lorrainer, Walcher, Prior of Malvern, wrote two astronomical works, the second of which was undoubtedly influenced by Arabic

114

writing, for instead of using the clumsy Roman fractions, he calculated in degrees, minutes and seconds. Adelard of Bath, early in the twelfth century, travelled widely in the East and possibly in Spain. He translated a number of books from the Arabic, the most important of which were Euclid's *Elements* and the *Liber Alchorismi*, a work by the Persian mathematician, Al-Khwarizmi, on the principles of arithmetic, geometry, music and astronomy. He also wrote original works, incorporating knowledge he had gained from Arab texts and also showing that questioning of authority which was characteristic of some of the bolder spirits of the time. Robert of Chester, a younger contemporary of Adelard, worked in Spain, as did Roger of Hereford later in the century. Most of these English scholars seem to have been primarily interested in Arabic mathematical and astronomical work. Daniel of Morley, who joined the school of translators established by Gerard of Cremona at Toledo, brought back with him to England a number of precious books, possibly translations of Aristotle and other Greek writers. Daniel then taught at the school of Northampton, which must have been a school of repute to attract a scholar of his standing. Other English scholars, like John of Salisbury, read Aristotle's logical books, which percolated into western Europe in the first half of the century. In the course of the twelfth century almost all the works of Aristotle and Ptolemy, the medical works of Hippocrates and Galen and the great medical *Canon* of the tenth-century Persian scholar, Avicenna, became available in Latin translations, together with the Arabic commentaries on them. Their influence on western scholars was evident, but its full effect was not felt until the next century, because this new knowledge from the ancient world and from the East was so staggering in its impact that it could not be immediately assimilated.

When our period opens, education in Europe was for clerks; it was in Latin and its content was suitable for monasteries and churches. A notable exception to this was pre-Conquest England, which had a vigorous and worthwhile literature in the old English language. In this field the coming of the Normans had a catastrophic effect. The English language was submerged as that of the conquered race. The French pattern of Latin as a written language and French as a spoken language applied on both sides of the Channel. The great bulge in the student population, which occurred in both England and France, was to have repercussions outside the schools. Literacy was becoming more widespread, especially in the upper classes, and among the women, who had no military preoccupations. In the old days the 'reading' of the ordinary lay folk, whether king or baron in his castle, squire in his hall, townsman or peasant in his tavern, was an aural exercise. The salaried minstrel, or the wandering minstrel, with his epic poetry or his lays, interspersed with music or dance, entertained the illiterate majority and, naturally enough, this kind of entertainment continued even when a slightly higher proportion of the laity could read. But the development of literacy did provide patrons and patronesses for written works in French and Norman French. The spoken epic was written down. The oldest manuscript of the Song of Roland is of this period and is in Oxford. There were also new stories and traditional folklore which found their way into prose and verse. To these stories England contributed her share or rather the Celtic fringe produced material which was to be woven into immortal stories, mostly by French writers. Geoffrey of Monmouth, in the early twelfth century, wrote in Latin his history of the *Kings of Britain*. This was translated into rhyming French couplets by the poet Wace in 1155 under the title of *Le Roman de Brut*, and so there crossed into France Arthur and his Round Table and the whole fairyland of Ireland, Wales, Cornwall and Brittany. The greatest name in poetry in England was Marie de France, a pseudonym which may conceal the Abbess of Shaftesbury and an illegitimate daughter of Henry II. She wrote both epics and lays. There were male poets writing of topical events or of the heroes of their time. Jordan Fantosme, a schoolmaster by profession, wrote a lively poem in French describing the capture of the King of Scotland in 1174. The fame of William the Marshal, Earl of Pembroke, was also perpetuated in French verse. But England's greatest contribution to the literature of the period was not in French but in Latin, not in verse but in prose. There were great chroniclers like William of Newburgh, Ralph of Diceto and Benedict of Peterborough and, in somewhat lighter vein, Jocelyn of Brakelonde, with his vivid picture of the Abbey of St Edmund under Abbot Samson. There was the historian of the fantastic, Geoffrey of Monmouth, and there were the satirists, Gerald of Wales and Walter Map. These are but a few of the numerous writers England produced in this period. The twelfth century was indeed an exciting period for those who could read and write.

Further Reading

A. F. Leach, *The Schools of Medieval England* [not very reliable but the only book on this topic]
C. H. Haskins, *The Twelfth Century Renaissance*
———, *Studies in the History of Medieval Science*
A. C. Crombie, *Augustine to Galileo. The History of Science* A.D. 400–1650
C. J. Webb, *John of Salisbury*

Scribe at work, from a MS. by Gerald of Wales

VII

Medicine and Law

Why were these two topics not included in the last chapter? They are university subjects today and there were schools of Medicine and Law in the twelfth century, increasingly so as the century wore on. The fact is that the medicine and law practised in this country were not the same as the medicine and law taught in the schools.

If the population of England in the mid-eleventh century was about one-and-a-half millions and in 1200 was possibly about two-and-a-half millions, this would mean that the numbers had rather less than doubled in one of the more expansive periods of the Middle Ages, when war took a limited toll and developing trade increased the demand for labour. The Black Death, in the mid-fourteenth century, was to wipe out about one third of the population. This was a major catastrophe, but lesser ones were a common occurrence in the Middle Ages. At a time when each agricultural year was self-contained, when man and beast depended on the crops and pasturage of the current season, when a bad winter, a too wet or too dry summer might leave the nation with insufficient basic foodstuffs to last until the next harvest, when whatever was the medieval equivalent of foot-and-mouth disease (it was called 'the murrain') might decimate

A not unusual deformity

118

the cattle population, it is not really surprising that famine was one of the recurrent hazards of medieval man. Famine, in its turn, bred pestilence, in that it lowered resistance to disease, and without adequate medical knowledge or medical care famine and pestilence took their toll of human life—and, incidentally, ensured that there was no unemployment problem.

Bathing a child in the all-purpose pot!

In the villages chronic inbreeding must have produced many children who started life with a built-in weakness, either mental or physical. Many would die in childhood, but others, who grew to manhood, might drag out a useless existence, dependent on charity for their sustenance. In general, infant mortality was extremely heavy. Probably the swaddling of babies, a universal custom, was an attempt to avert the common complaint of rickets. But once the child was free to crawl about among the insanitary rushes, with a child's natural instinct to put everything into its mouth, it is a wonder that any survived. From then on disease and accident would provide ample scope for a medical service, which was virtually non-existent. The earliest and ablest physicians we hear of were monks. Baldwin, who came from the Abbey of St Denis, near Paris, to be physician to Edward the Confessor, was rewarded by being made Abbot of St Edmund's. He continued in favour with William I and for the same reason. When he died in 1098 another abbot, Faricius of Abingdon, took his place as court physician and physician to the greater barons and clergy. Faricius was an Italian, and it is therefore possible that he had

Nurse and swaddled child

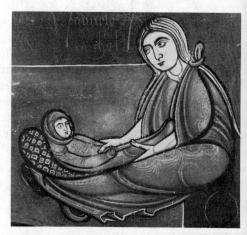

119

attended the medical school at Salerno, the only medical school in the Christian west in the eleventh century. There were monk physicians throughout the twelfth century. Some were simple monks and some abbots. Among the latter was Abbot Warin of St Albans, who used his medical knowledge to modify the curriculum of his monks in the interest of their health. Other monks, such as Walter, the almoner of St Edmund's, obviously practised outside the walls of their monasteries, and, equally obviously, took fees, for Walter was able to build an almonry with his, and Thomas, monk of Evesham, contributed to the building of the tower of his Abbey church in 1200. The monks were better placed than most others. Herbs, which were the basis of their medicine chests, could be grown in the monastery garden, money was not lacking to purchase such instruments as were available, and the monastery infirmary and almonry supplied them with unlimited material to practise on.

The scientific study of medicine made some progress in the twelfth century. Hippocrates and Galen were translated and used in the schools of Salerno and of Montpellier in southern France. But the best doctors were the Arabs, and it was not until the end of the twelfth century that the *Canon* of Avicenna was available in Latin. Lectures on medicine began in Paris at the end of the century, the lecturer being Giles of Corbeil, physician to Philip II of France, who was a product of the schools of Salerno and Montpellier. To help his students memorise the facts, Giles of Corbeil wrote his medical books in rhyme (*Incipit liber Magistri Aegidii de putribus metrice compositus*).

For England, as far as the twelfth century was concerned, medicine was traditional, composed of a mixture of herbal lore and popular magic, while surgery was brutal—and must often have been fatal. Two twelfth-century manuscripts, one early, show medical treatment, and in both cauterising looms large. The earlier one shows the physician cauterising a shorn head, while an attendant in a room below is heating a relay of instruments in a furnace. The second manuscript shows cauterising for trouble in the head and in the stomach—a painful remedy! In Trinity College, Cambridge, there is an illustrated medical treatise of the early thirteenth century, in which both text and pictures

Cauterising a shorn head. The servant below is heating further instruments of torture

Physician instructing his apprentice

show a more professional approach, with the physician dressed as became a member of a learned profession. There are illustrations of a trepan operation and of an abdominal one, and a number of vicious-looking eye operations. Two of the manuscripts show the doctor in his drug store, instructing his apprentice in the compounding of medicines. It was here that medieval superstition reigned supreme. The ingredients heated in the furnace and pounded in the mortar could contain anything from crushed rocks to entrails of animals and dead insects. Add to this complete credulity in regard to the malign or beneficent influence of certain planets and one is driven to the conclusion that the surest way to survive was to keep away from the doctor. In any case, most people would have no choice. The doctors' clientele was extremely limited. For ordinary folk, who could not afford to pay, there would be no doctor. Village folk would obviously depend on the ministrations and experience and the superstitions of the senior matrons of the community.

Three groups must have provided very common sights at this time—the lepers, the cripples and the blind. Provision for

Treating mumps (or toothache) and a cataract. This is early thirteenth century and the physician wears a professional look

A trepan operation—fee to be paid on the spot

lepers, who were the outcasts of society, was the motive for the foundation of many of the earliest hospitals, which were intended not for the cure of the sick but as a refuge for the incurable and the dying. Hospitals were not numerous in the twelfth century. Cripples were everywhere. When the only known way to deal with a leg wound, or other leg ailment, was to amputate, it stands to reason that anyone strong enough to survive the primitive and unanaesthetised severance of the limb would be joining a numerous band. Any crowd scenes depicted in twelfth-century manuscripts—and crowd scenes usually comprise a maximum of about ten persons—will almost invariably include at least one cripple. Crutches were common (*see* frontispiece) but wooden legs were not unknown.

Medieval man was smaller than his modern counterpart. Judging from surviving suits of armour, men averaged about five feet, five inches in height, and their womenfolk would be correspondingly shorter. Their life span was also generally much shorter than ours, although a few exceptions lived to a good old age. Men were considered old at 50. Henry II died as a very old man at 56, and he had been unusually strong and healthy.

The wooden leg

There were two great institutions

123

whose rapid development needed lawyers—the State and the Church. The only form of written secular law known to western Europe, with the exception of England, was Roman Law, which had been in the doldrums since the fall of the Western Roman Empire in the fifth century, but which took on a new lease of life in the late eleventh and early twelfth centuries, particularly in the great school of Bologna, in north Italy, under Irnerius and his successors. To this school came earnest men from all the countries of the West, whose careers demanded a knowledge of legal principles. The Church had its own law, which borrowed very heavily from Roman Law, and the Church, even more than the State, was turning to litigation as the remedy for all ills. Probably the most important date from the point of view of Canon (Church) law was the appearance about 1140 of Gratian's *Concordance of Discordant Canons*, more briefly known to everyone as the *Decretum*. It set out to arrange the material for the law of the Church, under headings and sub-headings, giving the numerous divergent opinions and, wherever possible, trying to reconcile them, by the method worked out by Peter Abailard in his teaching and his books. So, at a time when legal training was becoming essential for professional advancement in Church or State, the great Law School (later the University) of Bologna was flourishing, and other schools took up the teaching of law. It was for this professional qualification, more than any other, that the new generation of students, who were so strongly denounced by John of Salisbury, were prepared to scamp their preliminary humanist studies. There was, indeed, a legal renaissance in the twelfth century and it was a most important part of the Twelfth-Century Renaissance.

An Italian lawyer, Vacarius, whose greatest claim to fame is his book of Roman Law for Poor Students (the necessary teaching in the smallest possible compass), was in England during the reign of Stephen. He may have been a tutor to the young Prince Henry, later Henry II, when he was in the care of his uncle, Robert of Gloucester. We are told that he taught Roman Law at the school at Oxford. Then King Stephen, for reasons which are not entirely clear, forbade the teaching of

Roman Law in England. Although this decree seems to have been largely ineffective, most English ecclesiastics and lawyers (and most of the secular lawyers were ecclesiastics) got their schooling and their books abroad. In fact, although a knowledge of a logical system of law, such as Roman Law undoubtedly was, was most useful for our lawyers, English Law was to develop in its own way, and with very little logic about it, until, in the course of centuries, it became the great rival to Roman Law.

King and Council (or Witan)

From the Anglo-Saxon period we have laws, associated with the names of certain kings, and sponsored by their counsellors. These laws are unique for the period, as no other country in western Europe has anything like them. Many of them have come down to us in copies which were made in the early Norman period, especially in the reign of Henry I, and from that reign also we have an attempt at a textbook of English Law, called the *Quadripartitus* or *Four Parts*, although only two parts seem to have been written. William I and his successors claimed to be the legitimate heirs of the Saxon kings and they swore to

maintain the laws of the Kingdom: it was therefore essential
that they and their Norman lawyers should know what those
laws were. At the end of the twelfth century we have another,
and a very different, lawbook, *De Legibus Angliae*, in which the
author (traditionally thought to be the Justiciar Ranulf Glan-
ville) tries to describe the laws of England, at least of the king's
Court, as they are in his day, at the end of the reign of that
great lawyer, Henry II.

The Germanic peoples, when they settled in western Europe,
were primitive. Their kings were hardly more than leaders in
war, and there was little in the way of organised society. If one
man killed another, this started a blood feud between the kin
of the slain man and the slayer and his kin. A blood feud,
carried to its logical conclusion, could mean the virtual exter-
mination of the males of both kins. It was to avoid this wastage
of manpower that these peoples, including the Angles and
Saxons, had tried to substitute a system of tariffs for the feud.
Each man, according to his status in society, had his blood-price
or *wergild*. If he was slain, the killer and his kin could buy off the
feud by paying this *wergild* (200 shillings for an ordinary freeman in Wessex) to the dead man's kin, to be divided among
them according to an accepted scale. Personal injuries short of
death, seduction of one's wife or daughter and other matters,
which today come within the scope of the criminal law, were
all priced according to a tariff, which was given legal sanction
by the king and his counsellors, the Witan. Much of the body
of law which has come down to us is concerned with the details
of these tariffs—how much for a thumb, for a little finger, for a
big toe and other parts of the human anatomy. It was a matter
for settlement between the two families involved, but the settlement took place at a folk moot or meeting, usually the hundred
moot. The injured man or his family were responsible for
getting their adversary to court and for collecting the compensation (*bot*), if it was awarded them. The duty of the king's
officer was to preside over the meeting and to see that the
rules were kept. To him, as representing the king, was due a
fine (*wite*), which was paid by the loser. It was for the moot
to declare what form of proof the accused should undergo. For

a not too serious crime, or if the accused bore an exemplary character, he might be allowed to clear himself on oath, made in a set form of words before the altar of one or more churches. The moot also prescribed the number of oath helpers or compurgators, who had to swear before the same altars that he had sworn a true oath. Should any of them falter or make a mistake this was undeniable evidence that the deity declared he was guilty. It only remained to apply the appropriate part of the legal tariff and to leave the plaintiff to collect.

Other forms of invoking the judgement of God were the ordeals of cold or hot water or hot iron. In the case of cold water, the accused was thrown bound into the pond. If he sank he was innocent, but if the water rejected him and he floated he was guilty. The ordeal of hot water involved plunging the arm to the wrist or to the elbow, according to the judgement of the moot, and that of hot iron the carrying of one or three pounds of hot iron a prescribed distance. At the end of the ordeal the hand or arm was bandaged and if, after three days, it was healing nicely, its owner was innocent. Presiding over these orgies was a Christian priest, who had taken the place of a pagan priest of an earlier era. It was not beyond the bounds of possibility for the priest to be squared and for the judgement of God to be founded on something less than the prescribed temperature!

As the Anglo-Saxon kings became more powerful in the centuries leading up to the Norman Conquest so did the wite loom larger, and so also did the kings take a more active part in securing the peace of the country. They did this by insisting that every man should have a lord, who would guarantee his presence in court if necessary and pay the *bot* and *wer*, if he could not produce him; by grouping ordinary folk into 'tithings' (tens) responsible for the good behaviour of their members; and by taking into their personal peace or protection certain main roads, which we still refer to as the King's Highways. In spite, however, of the increasing part played by the State in what we should call the criminal law of the country, the basic idea on the eve of the Norman Conquest was compensation (*bot*) for the injured rather than punishment for the guilty. It is an idea which is slowly coming back into circulation today with tentative measures to compensate the victims of violence.

The Norman Conquest introduced a new element. For a new dynasty, established as the result of a ruthless conquest, it was a primary necessity to protect the alien intruders from the violence of the natives 'who would cut the throats of foreigners in woods and lonely places'. So police measures were tightened up, not by the introduction of a police force, which would have been inconceivable at that time, but by making sure that someone, whether lord or tithing (now called frankpledge) was responsible for dependants or members. For the security of the alien French a murder fine was introduced, and murder originally meant secret killing. If a body was found, the hundred in which it was found had either to prove that it was the body of an Englishman, or to produce the murderer, or to pay a communal fine. William decreed that Englishmen should be tried by English law and Normans by Norman law and this decree probably worked for a time, although, as courts did not keep records, it is difficult to be certain. What we do know is that references to *wergilds* and *bots* die out. Instead we get the strong arm of the king intervening in justice. We are told by the Peterborough Chronicle for the year 1124:

> In the same year, after St Andrew's Mass, before Christmas Ralph Basset and the king's thegns held a meeting of the Witan at Hundehoge in Leicestershire, and there hanged so many thieves as never were before, that was, in that little while, altogether four and forty men, and six men were deprived of their eyes. Many truthful men said there were many unjustly mutilated. A full heavy year it was.

An execution

Most probably the thieves hanged and mutilated were themselves of the conquered race.

The accent in the twelfth century was on law and this was true all over Europe, but in England under Henry I (35 years) and Henry II (35 years) and the great Justiciar of Richard I, Archbishop Hubert Walter, more and more people took more and more cases to the law courts instead of settling them, as they would have done previously, out of court with the help of relations and friends. In most criminal cases the courts would be the king's courts, either the royal court over which he often presided, or the local courts of shire and hundred, which acted in his name. But a number of great lords, particularly great churchmen, were responsible for justice over a wide area. For instance, the Bishop of Durham had his own courts for the whole of the Palatinate of Durham, and between them the Abbot of St Edmund's and the Bishop of Ely controlled almost all the courts of the large county of Suffolk. The king's court was itinerant. Wherever the king was there was the king's court and, at the very end of our period, in the last reign in which a king presided over a court of law, King John took a very personal part, giving, on the whole, fair judgement where lesser men were concerned but, it must be admitted, perverting justice to his own ends where his personal or political interests were at stake.

The executioner

One thing the kings and lords of the twelfth century did discover was that justice could be profitable, possibly more profitable than taxation. Fines were heavy and went to fill the Treasury. In some cases the lands and in all cases the chattels of an executed or an outlawed man went to the king, if the trial was in the king's court. We hear nothing now of compensation for the victims of violence or theft! Justice becomes retribution and from the twelfth century to the present day it has remained

129

so. In the old English period and in the early Norman period prisons were mainly for the great. For the ordinary offenders, fines, mutilation or death were simpler than keeping them in prison, but in 1166 Henry II ordered every sheriff to have a gaol and for this purpose he was permitted to cut trees in the king's forests or otherwise procure wood to build gaols in the king's castles and boroughs at the king's expense.

For in 1166 Henry II was making a great effort to round up the criminal population of the country, and he was doing it by making the leaders of the frankpledges (tithing groups) tell tales about their members to a jury of 12 men chosen from the hundred, who in their turn presented a list of the presumed offenders to the sheriff. Those so accused had to be kept in gaol by the sheriff until the king's justices came to the county or a neighbouring one. Then they submitted themselves to the judgement of God, which meant that the men went to the ordeal of cold water, the women and any freemen involved to the ordeal of hot iron. Whatever his subjects believed, Henry II was undoubtedly a sceptic. He decreed that if a man accused by his neighbours, and generally held in bad repute, was cleared by the ordeal, he must abjure the realm and leave with the first favourable wind. If the accused failed the ordeal he would lose his right foot. Ten years later Henry added the right hand for good measure. Some 574 criminals were condemned in 1166 and 705 in 1176, and their chattels, which went to the king, were valued at £655, quite a good haul for the Treasury in the money value of the time, but the average value of the chattels of each peasant so condemned seems to have been only ten shillings, a pathetic comment on his furnishings and equipment. In the reign of Henry II and his sons, the crafty wrongdoer could often avoid the worst consequences of his actions. A timely submission—putting himself in the king's mercy— would mean a fine and an escape from mutilation and outlawry and even from ordeal. In Lincoln in 1202, in about 430 cases of crime, including 114 cases of homicide, 89 of robbery (often with violence), 65 of wounding and 49 of rape, only two criminals were hanged and between 20 and 30 outlawed. Most of the others put themselves in mercy and paid fines, while some managed to reach sanctuary in a church, whence they would be allowed to go into outlawry. Most of the fines paid by boroughs, other communities and even individuals, were not for wrong-doing, but for not doing something which they probably did not know that they ought to do—for sins of omission rather than of commission: for, with the king's judges anxious to fill his, and their own, coffers, it was exceedingly difficult not to put a foot wrong.

The Durham sanctuary knocker

The Normans brought with them to England a form of trial customary on the continent, but not previously practised here—trial by battle, a reduction of the original feud to a fight between two men. It was again an appeal to supernatural judgement but, as with other ordeals, the odds were rarely even and there was the same tendency to put oneself in mercy and pay a fine. Until Henry II introduced his accusation by a jury of neighbours in 1166, most accusations were brought by the persons injured and the ordinary Norman way of doing this was a challenge to fight it out. Specific rules governed the contest. In the case of a criminal charge, the two must fight in their own persons unless one was a woman, an infant (i.e. under age), over 60 or maimed. In such a case a champion could be hired and there were enterprising capitalists who were prepared to hire out professional pugilists. Certain well-known and success-ful ones were very much in demand. We have an excellent description of trial by battle for homicide in an early thirteenth-century textbook of Norman law and, as the judicial duel was of Norman origin, we can probably rely on it for English pro-cedure, except for some variations of detail. There were many preliminaries and often many months spent before the champions actually met. Then the field was set, with four knights guarding the corners and the spectators, out for a half-day's holiday, sitting or standing in a ring round the outside. The champions

131

Trial by battle

wore padded jerkins, iron caps and wooden staves, possibly with steel tips. They came on to the field hand in hand, the one accusing the other of the crime and he retaliating with an accusation of perjury. Then they had to swear that they would not invoke the aid of demons and evil spirits. The preliminaries over, at noon they set to work, at first with their staves and, if these were broken, with fists, feet or teeth or any other part of the anatomy which could be put to use. It was up to the accuser to get the defendant down before the first star came out, otherwise he lost, and the loser had publicly to proclaim himself a murderer or perjurer or whatever kind of miscreant he was supposed to be.

It seems incredible that such superstitious practices should have survived and it is certain that those in authority in both Church and State were more than sceptical, but it was difficult for kings to break with the tradition of centuries, a pagan tradition carried over into the Christian era. It was left to the great pope Innocent III to settle the matter when, in 1216, he decreed that priests should no longer take part in the ordeal. This did not apply to the duel, in which priests were not involved, but even this became rarer and finally died out. The ordeals gave place in time to trial by jury. But England is not a methodical country. The old methods of trial were not abolished. They lapsed until, centuries later, in 1818, a young man 'appealed' his dead sister's fiancé of her murder and challenged him to a judicial duel, and he was within his legal rights to do so. At last the legislators got busy and since 1819 trial by battle has been illegal.

More important to the landowners than the changes in the criminal law were the changes in property law under Henry II and his successors. The one thing, above all others, which feudal courts had been competent to deal with was land law. If you

132

claimed that your neighbour had deprived you of your land, the case would be dealt with in the court of the overlord of that land. After long delays it would be decided by battle, fought by hired pugilists, for in civil cases the parties did not fight in person. Generally the man who had lost his land would take matters into his own hands, if he had force at his disposal and friends to back him up. This made for uncertainty and disorder, and the lawyer king, in the interests of order and his own pocket, took under his own protection the possession of land. The plaintiff would get from the king a writ, for which he had to pay, directing the sheriff of the county in which the land lay to empanel a jury of witnesses from the neighbourhood to speak the truth according to their knowledge. The new procedure was so effective that, before John died in 1216, a large proportion of cases involving property were being settled by it, and settled in the king's court, which was the only one competent to put witnesses on oath. Englishmen got the habit, which they have never lost, of taking their adversaries to court. The jury of witnesses was not like a modern jury. It did its homework and found out the facts before coming to court, but it, and similar bodies which were also set up by Henry II, pointed the way to an alternative method of trial when Pope Innocent III killed the ordeal in 1216.

Further Reading

J. F. Payne, *English Medicine in Anglo-Saxon Times*, 1904
F. Pollock and F. W. Maitland, *The History of English Law*, Vol. I, 1895
A. L. Poole, *Obligations* (*see* Chapter III)
T. F. T. Plucknett, *Early English Legal Literature*

VIII

The Building Crafts

The centrepiece of the medieval house was the hall. The domestic buildings of the monasteries were, in the main, the same as their secular counterparts, except that halls like the dorter and the frater were one-purpose halls, whereas the secular hall fulfilled a multitude of functions. Between the hall and the church there were very close links. They both derived from timber buildings. The timber hall, with its roof supported on twin rows of posts, is the parent both of the stone hall with wooden posts or stone pillars supporting the roof and dividing the space into nave and aisles, and of the stone church with pillars performing the same function. The nave of the aisled hall and of the early form of the aisled church closely resembled an upturned boat. The name 'nave' is derived from the Latin *navis*, a ship. The Germans still use the word *Schiff* for the nave of a church. As the masons grew more proficient in their use of stone and developed the ribbed vault, which enabled them more easily to

Oakham Hall, Rutland: the interior

roof great spaces, so church architecture drew away from domestic, but this process had not gone very far before the end of the twelfth century. Therefore the stone church and the stone hall share this chapter.

The Normans had a very good building stone, the famous white stone of Caen, and, when means permitted, it was used for some of the finer building work in England, for instance for the choir of Canterbury Cathedral in 1175. But there were parts of England where suitable stone could be quarried, the best being within the belt of Jurassic limestone outcrop, which crosses England from the Cleveland Hills in Yorkshire to Lyme Regis in the South-West. It includes much of Lincolnshire and the neighbourhood of Peterborough in the East, and in the West the Cotswolds and Oxford, where the Headington quarries later provided the stone for the Oxford colleges. Towards the end of the twelfth century the famous Purbeck marble came into use for the slender decorative columns characteristic of the new style of architecture, which was then developing in England. If English stone was being used at a distance from the quarries, it, like the stone of Caen, would be cut to pattern at the quarry. If local stone was used then blocks would be quarried and the actual shaping and dressing done on the building site.

The period of 30 years or so after the Norman Conquest is sometimes known as the Anglo-Saxon overlap, because the Norman talent in the form of Norman masons seems to have been in inadequate supply. The English masons, if left to them-

Tewkesbury Abbey, Gloucestershire: the Norman nave

135

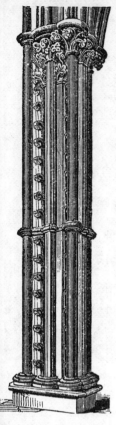

Purbeck column, Lincoln Cathedral, c. 1200

selves, applied their own techniques. The king obviously employed Norman masons and engineers (much the same) and carpenters because such are found, with Norman names, in Domesday Book as direct tenants of the king. Among them were Waldin the Engineer and Radbell the Artificer, with quite substantial holdings. Durand the Carpenter held the manor of Moulham in the parish of Swanage and that of Afflington near by. He may well be the ancestor of the de Moulham family, which existed as late as Elizabeth I. The title engineer was applied to one who built not only siege engines (mangonels, trebuchets, catapults and the rest) but also the buildings in which or against which they were used. The king could use his engineers on any work in which he was interested. Ailnoth *Ingeniator* supervised work at Westminster Abbey when the frater had to be rebuilt. The first people who were involved in a great stone building project were the masons, and there must have been a master mason who saw the building as a whole. Of actual plans of buildings we have none for our period. Either they never existed or they were not preserved. It was purposeless to preserve them. Parchment was expensive and they could be erased. The building was always marked out on the ground. Measurements seem to have been none too precise. It is said that in a vision St Thomas the Apostle and St Thomas the Martyr ordered a chapel to be built in their honour at Devizes. They measured it out with their feet, one with the right foot only and the other with both. One measured 12 feet and the other 13. Many country churches show irregularities which may easily be due to a variable measuring unit, such as the human foot, on the ground.

The master mason lacked the technical training and knowledge of the modern architect, but he had one advantage. He had started as an apprentice and had learnt his craft by practising it. He could, and often did, take a hand in the actual construction work. The masons were unlike most other craftsmen. Not many

136

could find permanent work in any one neighbourhood. The king, and perhaps the greater cathedrals and abbeys, might retain the services of a master mason and even a skeleton staff, but in general when building operations were in progress masons would be brought in from outside. Henry III, when he wanted a job finished quickly, was not above impressing labour, skilled and unskilled, although he paid well for it. It is more than probable that his ancestors did the same, although proof is lacking.

Master mason discussing plans with the king

Unemployed masons, hearing of work in a certain place, would journey there and report to the masons' lodge, the temporary local headquarters of the craft. Here, in a wooden building, the masons were engaged, lived and did such work as dressing stones, which could be done on the site but not on the building itself. There were various kinds of masons, the rough hewers, who quarried the stone, the superior masons who worked it for ashlar—building blocks—and those who actually laid the stone. Subsidiary to them were the mortarmen, barrowmen and others. Until almost the end of the twelfth century, beyond it in some cases, the elaborate carving was part of the mason's work, probably because in Romanesque architecture, which we also call Norman, sculpture and carving were an integral part of the building. The main tool of the mason was his axe, either the two-bladed axe or the hammer axe, with which he seems to have executed most of the carvings until about the mid-twelfth century, if Gervase of Canterbury is to be believed

Carrying earth or stone in a wicker hod

137

Carving with axe (c. 1110) and chisel (c. 1180) at Canterbury

when he writes, apropos of the rebuilding of the Canterbury choir about 1180, that the new capitals and arcades were carved with the chisel whereas the older ones had been carved with the axe. With the change from Romanesque and the development of a sculpture independent of the building, a new artist in stone appears—the imager.

Stone lore was as well known to the medieval mason as to his successor today. He knew that the lower layers in quarries were better than the upper, which could be used for rubble. He knew also that stone should be orientated in the building as it was in the quarry. Stones were sometimes set in the wrong way of the grain and this tended to weaken the building. Alexander Neckham, writing in 1200, describes the steps in building from the foundation to the top of the wall, using level and plumbline, but he states that the walls must not be parallel. They must radiate from the

Building craftsmen at work

Builders in c. 1180, with mason using chisel

centre of the earth (obviously a spherical earth!). A drawing, probably by Matthew Paris in the mid-thirteenth century,
can be taken as representing similar activities at an earlier
date, for techniques changed very slowly. It shows all sorts
of machines and tools. Masons are dressing stones on the
site with the axe. An earlier manuscript, of 1180, shows similar
tools, but in this case the chisel is the instrument for dressing
the stone. St Hugh, Bishop of Lincoln, when his great cathedral was in building, would carry the hods of stone or lime with
the meanest of his workers.

If the stone masons formed a fluid labour force and their
lodges were mainly temporary, the carpenters were, with few
exceptions, able to work on a permanent local basis. As almost
all houses, and even some castles and a few churches, were still of
wood, and as stone buildings mostly required timber for roof
and towers, there was a regular and widespread demand for
carpenters. They were also needed, of course, on all shipbuilding.

The timber was of oak where possible, but unfortunately it
was not always well chosen. Owing to the cost of transport the
tendency was to cut down the nearest trees and quite often use

Shipbuilding

the wood immediately. Being unseasoned it was liable to warp, and, although an effort was made to counteract this by using timbers uneconomically and unaesthetically massive, some surviving medieval buildings show irregularities that were certainly not intended. In spite of the cost, some careful builders went to great lengths to procure the timber of their choice. Abbot Faritius of Abingdon, in the early twelfth century, sent to Wales for the beams and rafters of his abbey. It was an expensive business, for it needed six waggons each with 12 oxen, and the journey to and from Shrewsbury took from six to seven weeks.

The timber roof was merely a framework on which could be laid a waterproof covering, thatch, shingles, lead or tiles. For ordinary buildings thatch was the most usual, and very dangerous it proved. It would be impossible to give a list of the great fires caused by thatch, not only from external sparks but from the domestic fires, usually in the centre of the room, which could ignite roof timbers and thatch. London was devastated by fire in 1077, 1087, 1161, and in many other years, and other towns suffered similarly, but it was not until 1212 that the authorities tried to do something about it and then

Greenstead, Essex: most of the church has been rebuilt, but the heavy nave timbers are original

only for London. No roofs in future were to be covered with reeds, sedge, straw or stubble, but with tiles, shingle, boards, lead or plastered straw, and all existing roofs of reed or sedge were to be plastered. Tiles seem to have been rarely used until the thirteenth century and then to have been imported from Flanders. Shingles—tiles of oak—were common in the better buildings. Even Henry III used shingle roofs extensively.

Working on a shingle roof

Lead had many advantages, including the possibility of being recast and re-used, but it was expensive and it was mined in only a few parts of the country. Many of the mines belonged to the king, and the miners were a privileged community, although they were often 'pressed' to work in the mines. The mining town of Alston, in the northern Pennines, could not have been self-supporting. Its bleak moors could have produced little or no arable land, but the neighbouring vills had the duty of providing the necessary food. The king might lease his mines, as he leased Alston to the Bishop of Carlisle, or he might claim the product for himself, have it carted to the nearest waterway and then transported by sea. Lead for the roofs, gutterings, etc. of cathedrals, abbeys and other churches ranked high among the king's gifts to these institutions. For roofing the lead was not laid directly on the timber, because the vegetable acids in wood, particularly if unseasoned, adversely affected the lead, and in extremes of temperature the lead could also affect the timber, so earth, sand or moss was laid on the timber before it was leaded. The collecting of this insulating material was work often done by women.

The windows in the greater churches were generally glazed and in the twelfth century the glass was sometimes richly coloured, but in smaller churches and in domestic buildings, including royal ones, the windows were openings in the wall, intended to let in light with as little ventilation as possible. As most rooms opened directly to the outer air there was little need

141

Window seat at Millichope Park, Shropshire

for ventilation. The window openings could be covered with a grid for security, or with oiled linen or canvas to exclude draught without entirely excluding light, or closed completely by shutters during the hours of darkness. In stone buildings the windows were splayed so that the outer opening was narrow and the inner one at least twice the width. This was easy because of the thickness of the walls. It made for security and it enabled the small amount of light to fan out inside the room and illumine a greater area.

In spite of this it would be impossible, even if desired, to do embroidery or to read inside the room. It was therefore not unusual to have stone seats along the thickness of the wall in the window opening.

Not everyone could get up with the sun and retire to bed on its setting, so some form of artificial lighting was necessary. The most usual form was candlelight. The candlemakers or 'candlewrights' had their own street in London, giving its name to Candlewick Ward. Candles, or more often candle ends, were part of the daily ration of members of the king's household. The candle was supported on a candlestick, which was literally a spike or stick, not a socket. Candlesticks might be severely practical or they might, as today, aspire to artistic merit. A cheaper, usually home-made light, was made from peeled rushes soaked in fat.

Fourteenth-century open hearth (at Penshurst Place, Kent), in use until recently

Heating was a problem in the Middle Ages as now. For all ground-floor halls and for cottages the normal was a hearth and a log or peat fire in the centre of the floor. There is no evidence of paving in houses during this period, although it is possible that a raised dais for the lord's table was paved. Generally the floor was of trodden earth, covered with rushes

142

or straw. The logs might rest on irons and the smoke would find its way up into the rafters and out through either a simple hole in the roof, a hole with a bottomless barrel inserted or a more elaborate louvre, that would help protect the fire below from the rain above. Modifications in the few existing ground-floor halls have done away with the open hearth. The illustration shows a fourteenth-century hearth, in use until quite recently. It is possibly more elaborate than the earlier type, but one can imagine the effect of such a fire in a draughty room. In stone keeps, and in fact in any room raised above ground level and therefore likely to have a wooden floor—and in the case of the keep a ceiling rather than a roof above—the central hearth was clearly impossible. The first wall fireplaces were in keeps (*see* p. 34). They were set in the thickness of the wall, with vents in the sides of the flat buttress. In first-floor halls and later in chambers, the fireplace was often hooded and the smoke carried away by a chimney, usually round. In the matter of heating the monasteries were behind the secular world. The only fire was in a special room, the calefactory. Of course kitchens had to have fires and there the monasteries, with their all-the-year-round cooking demands, were in advance of secular habitations, where the kitchens were often primitive shacks and the cooking was sometimes done in the open.

Tied up with the question of kitchens is that of water supply. Streams or ponds

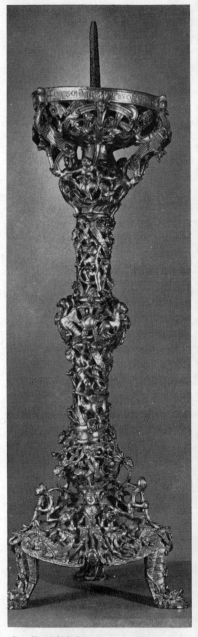

Candlestick belonging to Serlo, Abbot of Gloucester, late eleventh century

143

Round chimney at Christchurch, Hampshire

were the obvious answer and there was no thought of purifying the water before use. Big establishments might have wells and these were essential in castles, almost impregnable to attack, but vulnerable if their food or water supply ran out. Usually the well was fitted with windlass and bucket, but a few seem to have had a dipping beam and counterweight. London had its first public water supply in 1237. As regards sanitation, apparently kitchen refuse was just thrown out or carried to the nearest stream. It was not until 1260 that a conduit was made to carry the refuse of the king's kitchens at Westminster to the Thames. Hitherto it had been carried through the halls and the stench had affected the health of the people attending the Court. For other necessary sanitation cesspits were the normal answer and apparently not all builders placed them sufficiently far from the houses. In fact in towns it is doubtful whether they could always do so. In castles the privies were usually in the thickness of the walls, with shoots leading to the foot of the walls or corbelled out. Again the monastery, as a large, permanently resident community, led the way both in water supply and in sanitation. Eating habits, in which fingers took the place of modern cutlery, made handwashing be-fore and after meals most desirable, but for monks it was decreed by their Rule. There was always a *lavatorium* in the cloister; near the entrance to the refectory. There was also provided in association with each dormitory or dorter a *necessarium* or rere-dorter. A monastery was usually so arranged that its *necessarium* could drain into or be flushed by a stream. Much ingenuity was displayed in the Middle Ages, as now, to find a polite term for these places. Privy was the most common, but for the king the term *garderobe*, usually translated 'wardrobe', but equally correctly 'cloakroom', suggests a euphemism still in use today.

Hooded fireplace, Boothby Pagnell

144

The most extraordinary feat of planning in this respect occurred at Canterbury under Prior Wibert, who died in 1167. Here was a conduit house close to the source of supply and from this ran an underground pipe, which passed through five long reservoirs or settling tanks, each with a flushing device where the water entered it, to the city wall and so to the monastery. It fed the lavers in the infirmary cloister and outside the refectory by means

Well with dipping beam and counterweight

of raised cisterns, which enabled the water to trickle continuously into the washing basins below. The pipes also fed the brewhouse, bakery, almonry and bath-house and the Prior's private bath-house. There was a branch line which may have been for the use of the City of Canterbury. Joined by the waste from the bath-house, the water passed into a main drain, which flushed the *necessarium* and then passed under the City wall into the City ditch. At convenient points, as for the kitchens, there were standpipes with cocks. The system was most efficient and remained almost unchanged until the dissolution of the monastery in the sixteenth century. Although this was by far the most elaborate system in the twelfth century and for some centuries after, other monasteries attempted a controlled water supply. St. Edmund's, in 1200, brought its water two miles in underground lead pipes.

One other craft was concerned, though less fundamentally perhaps, with building. Locks and bolts, hinges, fancy iron gates and grilles and, of course, nails brought in the ironworkers. The greater barons would have their smiths to deal with the swords and other weapons of themselves and their men. There were smiths in a large proportion of the villages and in the towns, but the majority of them would be dealing with the more pedestrian tasks of their craft, such as shoeing the wooden

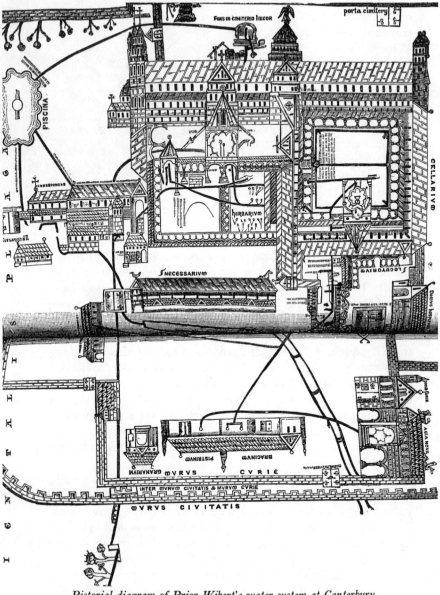

Pictorial diagram of Prior Wibert's water system at Canterbury

A baron's smiths at work

shovels and other tools with iron—iron was too scarce for tools to be made entirely of the metal. Gloucester was a centre of the iron industry and in 1172 it supplied 25,000 nails for the king's house at Winchester. Hinges on the heavy doors were large and ornate. Keys and keyholes were obviously known, but Alexander Neckham prescribes padlocks: 'let every door have a pensile lock'.

The vast building programme, embracing castles, palaces and manor houses, cathedrals, abbeys, nunneries, parish churches and hospitals, made of the late eleventh and the twelfth centuries as exciting a period as our vast building projects are making today. For ecclesiastical building the benefaction and the motive force came often from kings and secular lords, who thus expressed their piety or their pride in stone. William I commemorated his victory at Hastings by founding Battle Abbey, Henry I's favourite foundation was at Reading and Stephen's was Faversham, but William II is represented by his great secular building, Westminster Hall. It was, however, the great abbots and bishops who were predominantly responsible for the magnificent abbeys and cathedrals. Where there were Anglo-Saxon buildings, the tendency was to destroy and build anew and even these new buildings did

Ironwork on the door of Staplehurst Church, Kent

147

Royal builders: (top) William I, Battle Abbey;
William II, Westminster Hall; (bottom)
Henry I, Reading Abbey; Stephen, Faversham
Abbey

not always escape the destroyer, for the great churchmen wanted always the latest style and the most imposing.

'This year [1093] in the presence of almost all the bishops and abbots of England, on 8 April, with great joy and honour, the monks came from the old monastery at Winchester to the new. On the feast of St Swithin a procession was formed from the new monastery to the old and they brought the shrine of St Swithin and placed it in the new church. Next day, by order of Bishop Walkelin, men began to break up the old monastery; and it was all broken up in that year except one chapel and the high altar.'

The tower of Walkelin's new building fell in 1107: some said because William II, the eleventh-century anti-Christ, had been buried under it; others, more sceptical, blamed the inadequacy of the foundations. A new tower was built and joined to the old work, and the junction gives us the chance to see how much the masons had progressed in skill between the two dates.

Archbishop Lanfranc, appointed to Canterbury in 1170, had no need to pull down the old church, for soon after the Conquest

> the City of Canterbury was set on fire by the carelessness of some persons, and the rising flames caught the mother church thereof . . . and the whole was consumed. . . . [Lanfranc] pulled down to the ground all that he found of the burnt monastery, whether of buildings or the wasted remains of buildings and having dug out their foundations from under the earth, he built in their stead others which greatly excelled them in beauty and in size.

148

Perhaps it was as well that abbots and bishops wanted, wherever possible, to destroy the old and start from scratch. The task of welding old and new seems to have been beyond the skill of most medieval masons, or perhaps if it was a case of modification the resident mason was considered adequate and the more skilled specialist from outside was not called in. At Abingdon in 1091 the Abbot decided to enlarge the sanctuary of the old church. A chapel was taken down and the existing tower had to be linked to the new building. In doing this the masons disturbed the foundations of the tower and 'on Friday, 28 March [1091] while the brethren were attending nightly service in the place where the Chapter was held and had just finished the third lesson, the tower fell in a marvellous manner'. Marvellous indeed, for the Prior seems to have had some premonition of danger and had removed the service from church to chapter house.

The great buildings which look so immensely strong to us are the survivals. A number of towers suffered the fate of those of Abingdon and Winchester. Sometimes they fell without obvious reason: often it was the inadequacy of the foundations; sometimes the disaster was attributed to what our legal system calls 'Act of God', in other words, storm and tempest. It seems incredible that buildings, even remotely resembling those which have survived from the Norman period, should have been unable to withstand storms, which in all probability were no worse than we have occasionally had in the twentieth century. The answer must be that the majority of masons were very average craftsmen, unable to make up by inspiration for their lack of mathematical and engineering knowledge. It is also certain that then, as now, workmen not closely supervised might scamp their work. Be that as it may, towers, including those of St Edmund's, Chichester (two) and Evesham, were blown down. We have a contemporary description of a storm in London in 1091.

At this time also, winds, blowing from all quarters in a way marvellous to relate, began on 17 October to blow so violently that they shattered more than 600 houses in London; churches were reduced to heaps, as also houses, stone walls like those of timber. . . .
The fury of the wind lifted up the roof of the Church of St Mary,

which is called at Bow, and crushed two men there. Rafters and beams were carried through the air, and of these rafters four of 26 feet in length, when they fell in the public street, were driven with such force into the ground that they scarcely stood out four feet, and as they could in no way be pulled out, orders were given to cut them off level with the ground.

Fire was another constant hazard and an opportunity for the ambitious builder. One church which seems to have suffered more than its due share from fire was Christchurch, Canterbury. Lanfranc found it destroyed by fire and rebuilt it. In 1109, 20 years after his death, Prior Ernulf 'rebuilt the fallen west end of the church, which Lanfranc had erected, so magnificently that nothing of the kind could be seen in England for its blaze of glass windows, for its glitter of marble paving and its paintings of many hues'. Clear evidence that our English churches were once as gay as those of southern Europe! The Church was completed by Prior Conrad 'who adorned it with noteworthy painting'. All this was doomed to a short survival. 'In the year of grace 1174, by the just but occult judgement of God, the Church of Christ at Canterbury was consumed by fire, to wit that glorious choir which had been so magnificently completed by the industry of Prior Conrad.' Apparently towards the end of September in that year, during a gale force wind, three cottages outside the monastery walls were destroyed by fire. The onlookers could do nothing and went home. Meanwhile the high wind had carried cinders and sparks to the roof of the church and the wind drove them between the rafters. From there the fire spread to the main beams, not noticed because it was between the painted ceiling and the lead roof. 'And now that the fire had loosened the beams from the pegs which bound them together, the half-burnt timbers fell into the choir below upon the seats of the monks: the seats, consisting of a great mass of woodwork, caught fire, and thus the mischief grew worse and worse. And it was marvellous, though sad, to behold how that glorious choir itself fed the fire that was destroying it.' The monks were heartbroken and for a time did nothing, using the undamaged nave for their services, but ultimately they began to take advice from English and French craftsmen, finally choosing a Frenchman,

William of Sens, because of his great reputation.

William was an architect in that he made the overall plan, he was a master mason in that he actually took part in the work. He also arranged for the shipment of the white stone of Caen, cut and dressed in the quarries to wooden patterns to save transport. He also devised machinery for loading and unloading the stone and for lifting it. He seems to have been a universal genius, but 'in the beginning of the fifth year, he was in the act of preparing with machines for the turning of the great vault, when suddenly the beams broke under his feet and he fell to the ground, stones and timber accompanying his fall, from the height of the capitals of the upper vault, that is to say 50 feet'. Poor William! He was now bedridden and tried to direct the work from his bed, through the agency of a certain ingenious and industrious monk. But medieval medicine was less advanced than medieval architecture and, finding that he gained no benefit from the physicians, William gave up the work and returned to his home in France. 'And another succeeded him in charge of the work: William by name, English by nation, small in body but in workmanship of many kinds acute and honest.'

Canterbury choir, by William of Sens

Christchurch, Canterbury, was the primatial church of England. At the other end of the ecclesiastical ladder was the small Abbey of Meaux, founded about 1150 by the Earl of Albemarle. 'He caused to be erected a great building, though of wretched masonry, . . . so that the convent should come and dwell therein

Christchurch, Canterbury: outside staircase to guest house

until he should make more convenient arrangements for them. He made also a chapel beside the said building, where all the monks used to sleep in the lower solar and in the upper they devoutly celebrated divine service.' This is clearly the type of two-storey building, often constructed in stone in the twelfth century, to accommodate a chamber on the first floor and a storehouse below, and having an outside stairway. This building soon proved too small. One can imagine the monks at Meaux as sleeping somewhat uncomfortably in the cellar. Abbot Adam and his monks then erected another building, from the planks which had come from William Fossard's castle at Montferrant, which had been destroyed by the king's orders, obviously one of the many motte-and-bailey type castles, with wooden keep, erected in large numbers by the warring barons in Stephen's reign and whose destruction was ordered by his successor. Abbot Philip (1160–82) began a new church, which his successor Abbot Thomas pulled down, 'because it was unsatisfactory in plan and construction. But afterwards his successor, Alexander, the fourth abbot [1197–1210] destroyed this same new building and began to build afresh the existing church.' Five new churches in a little more than half a century! The second was of wood, the first and presumably the last of stone. Of the other two we know nothing. It is probable that this sort of thing was happening all over the country. When we know about it, it is not from the survival of the old fabric, but from the chronicles which were kept by most monasteries in the twelfth century.

It is, however, to the survivors of the great churches that we turn to remind ourselves of the magnificent achievements of

Durham Cathedral: the nave, 1099–1133

Norman England, to cathedrals still in daily use like Durham, Peterborough, Ely and Lincoln, and to majestic ruins like Fountains (*see* p. 100), Rievaulx and Tintern, medieval skyscrapers, 'towers threatening the stars' (*turres sideribus minantes*), as Alexander Neckham called them.

The final touch to a medieval building, as to this chapter, was the weathercock or vane, which could be useful or ornamental or both. The setting of the weathercock on the Confessor's Abbey of Westminster symbolises in the Bayeux Tapestry the completion of the building.

Further Reading

D. Knoop and G. P. Jones, *The Medieval Mason*, 1933
L. F. Salzman, *Building in England down to 1540*, 1952
S. O. Addy, *The Evolution of the English House* (ed. Summerson), 1933
A. W. Clapham, *Romanesque Architecture in England*, 1950

*Putting the weathercock
on Westminster Abbey*

IX

Arts and Entertainments

In Anglo-Saxon England most of the workers in what may be
called the artistic crafts were monks. Their work in metals and
precious stones was finer than anything their conquerors could
produce. After the Conquest professional lay craftsmen took
over the work of the monks and for a time quality undoubtedly
suffered, but the second generation of Norman abbots and
bishops, although they were not craftsmen themselves, began,
under the leadership of such men as Abbot Serlo of Gloucester
(*see* p. 143) and Henry of Blois, Abbot of Glastonbury and Bishop
of Winchester, to show appreciation of works of art, to collect
them on their travels and to give their patronage to native
craftsmen. Of course, there were still some gifted monks, who
were able to enrich their monasteries with the work of their
hands. Probably the greatest of these was Hugh, Sacrist of the
Abbey of St Edmund, who was
responsible not only for the
marvellous illumination of the
famous Bury Bible, but who
carved the screen and cast the
bronze doors and the bell of the
church. Another artcraft in which
Anglo-Saxon England was pre-
eminent was that of embroidery.
Much of it, of course, was
ecclesiastical, the garments of
officiating priests being liberally
embroidered; the king and the

Henry of Blois, Bishop of Winchester

155

An ivory crozier

wealthier nobles would also have embroidered bands on their tunics. Ladies of noble birth were often adept at stitchery and they, with their women, may have been responsible for the actual embroidery, although they worked to designs of such masters of drawing as the illuminators of some of the Anglo-Saxon manuscripts.

The most famous piece of embroidery which has survived, probably from the third quarter of the eleventh century, is that which is traditionally, though not accurately, known as the Bayeux Tapestry. It is an embroidered strip of linen, what survives being about 80 yards long. The embroidery is in wool, in eight colours, and its theme the relations between Harold Godwinson and Duke William, from the mission of Harold to Normandy in the last years of Edward the Confessor to the death of Harold and the flight of the English at the Battle of Hastings. It has a narrow border of embroidery at the top and bottom, mainly decorative, with strange birds and some fables. Expert opinion today tends to the view that it was commissioned by William's brother, Bishop Odo of Bayeux, possibly in connection with the consecration of his new cathedral at Bayeux in 1077, that the embroideresses who worked it were English from Odo's Earldom of Kent, and that they worked to a design created by an artist of very considerable talent, who may also have been English. He was clearly a man familiar with the art of book illumination as practised in pre-Conquest England. The Bayeux Tapestry provides us, in the form of an outsize strip-cartoon, with illustrations of contemporary armour, Norman and English, of civilian clothing, of boat building and navigation, of kitchen and table customs, of fighting, of castles and houses and the Confessor's Abbey of Westminster. From the social historian's point of view it is an invaluable record and from the art historian's it is a magnificent achievement and the sole survivor of its kind from the period. We have only fragments of ecclesiastical embroidery from the twelfth century, but we know of the existence of elaborate work, both secular and ecclesiastical, from descriptions and pictures.

One of the first and most fundamental arts of the time was handwriting. Printing was still more than two centuries in the future when our period ends. There was no means of duplication except by the slow and painful method of copying. Most of the writing was done on prepared animal skins, which, fortunately for us, have withstood the ravages of time as our modern paper would not have done. But animal skins were not in unlimited supply and the finer parts used in the production of the great Bibles and missals were still rarer. Less important works had to be content with the offcuts and we constantly find holes in them, obviously original holes as there are no breaks in the

Embroidered buskin, found in the tomb of Archbishop Hubert Walter (d. 1205)

text. Many valuable works have been erased, by scraping, so that the skin could be re-used. Because of the shortage of material, handwriting got smaller and letters closer and some words were abbreviated. In Anglo-Saxon England handwriting was not a professional craft. Books were produced in monasteries. They were works of love and devotion, whether religious texts or secular books, such as the Anglo-Saxon Chronicle. After the Conquest, the monasteries continued to be the main centres of book production, but some of them found that they could not meet all their needs without employing paid labour. The professional copyist was creeping in.

With the increasing demand for books, particularly in the twelfth century, there developed a profession of writers, working on a commercial basis, such as there had been in the Roman

157

INCIPIT LIBER PRIMUS TRANSLATIONIS SCI
AUGUSTINI ANGLORUM APLI · ET SOCIO.
RUM EIUS ·

OST ANTIQUA
EVANGELICI PROTO
PARENTIS ANGLO
RU AUGUSTINI

folennia celo triumphata que nup eginnuf laude
feftiua: noua nob ouc gta. noua letiria. folennitaf
noua. Ipfa eft fua fcoroq: collegarum fuor cnflatio
noua: que p cencu fere luftra in noua ei facta ia lucec
eccla. In priou fefto de fcli agone & cenebrif ad folem
ote palmat afcendic. mifto de diucho humi ergaftu

Monkish hand

Empire. The best books and the finest writing were still the
work of monks, but ordinary books were made by paid scribes
and sold by booksellers, always to be found in the vicinity of the
great schools of the century. According to Peter of Blois they
were not above turning a dishonest penny and were anything
but reliable. Handwriting deteriorated, mistakes multiplied and
so did abbreviations until we have in effect a medieval Latin
shorthand. Separate works were often bound together. When a
scribe finished his text he occasionally relieved his feelings and
his boredom by scribbling, in Latin, at the end, a favourite
recipe—for salad, for face cream, for making sour ale sweet—or
even a heartfelt 'Thank God, that is finished! Now I can go and
get a drink'. In spite of its deterioration, the book hand of the
twelfth century remains fairly legible. Towards the end of the
century it was beginning to change. Writers were introducing
flourishes: they were forming pointed letters with thin up-
strokes and thick downstrokes, a handwriting which was to be
known as Gothic and which is far more difficult to read than the

simpler, rounded type. Ordinary business documents were written in a cursive hand, in which the stroke was carried on from one letter to the next. It is quicker and easier to write but more difficult to read.

The monks took pride not only in their handwriting but in the illumination of their books and this had achieved a high degree of perfection before 1066. Illumination had two purposes—decoration and illustration. The great decorative initials were usually in colour. Other pictures could be coloured but were sometimes line drawings, entirely black and white or outlined in colour. The Anglo-Saxon monks were capable of producing not only beautiful but also very vivid pictures. Book illuminations suffered a temporary setback after the Conquest, as the new Norman prelates were more interested in building than in the work of pen and brush. From the late eleventh century we have mainly historiated initials with intense colour, but the twelfth century saw a very rapid development in pictorial art, and this was not confined to books.

Of this development, as of so many phases of medieval life, the Church was the active centre. It had on its hands the problem of making its liturgy, its biblical doctrine and its moral teaching intelligible to an illiterate laity, and a laity which did not even understand the spoken language of the church service. This demanded visual aids. Two of these were sculpture and painting in the churches themselves. A third grew out of the liturgy and it dates back beyond the eleventh century.

The twelfth-century sculptures were part of the structure, the work of the mason rather than of the imager. The tympanum, the semicircular space between the door and the arch above, provided the best

St George and the dragon: tympanum at Brinsop, Herefordshire

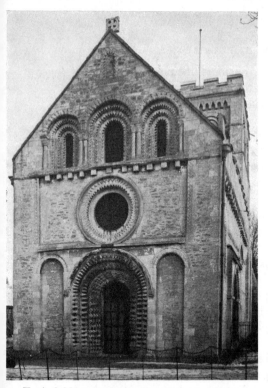

Typical Norman dog-tooth ornament: Iffley, Oxfordshire

opportunity for picture sculpture: the craftsman, an illiterate who could still appreciate pictures in books, probably drew inspiration from these. For the first 80 years or so after the Conquest, except for the dog-tooth ornament which was so common a feature of Anglo-Norman architecture, much of the work was plain and the carving somewhat crude, the work of pick and axe rather than of chisel. Some of the plain capitals of the period have been carved since.

The surviving churches, with their solidity, their small splayed windows and general air of sobriety and even dourness, can give us little notion of their appearance when they were built. All, great and small alike, were plastered and painted. William of Malmesbury wrote: 'We think it not enough . . . unless the walls glisten with various coloured paintings and throw the reflection of the sun's rays upon the ceiling'. The general scheme seems to have been that the roof represented the sky and was painted with the celestial bodies— stars, moon and other planets. The nave, occupied by the laity, showed the earthly life of Christ, the Virgin Mary and the saints, while figures of saints or personified Virtues could be painted on the window splays. The chancel represented heaven after the Last Day and the chancel arch the gateway to heaven, often with a vision of the Last Judgement. On the under-side of the arch, the soffit, could be represented the succession of the seasons with the labours of the various months, labour being the world's heritage from Adam. To crown all, above the high altar, would be the outsize figure of Christ in majesty. Gervase of Canterbury tells us that Lanfranc's choir was painted with a heaven. Clearly there would be variations on the theme and great churchmen, like St Bernard of Clairvaux, strongly objected to pictures of animals and grotesque figures in churches. The Virtues and Vices, fighting battles in which the Virtues always triumphed, was a favourite theme. It is possible that the outsides of many churches were painted but there is no surviving evidence from this country.

What we have left of the inside work is, of course, a small fraction of what was once there. The natural life span of such paintings would not be more than about 150 years, but an even greater hazard was the ease with which they could be obliterated and the church brought up to date. Any survivors were either destroyed or plastered over by the iconoclast Puritans in the seventeenth century. Some have been uncovered in comparatively recent times, but the removal of overlying plaster is itself a tricky operation and the paintings so revealed are then subject to the ordinary process of attrition. The best preserved are at Canterbury, in St Gabriel's and St Anselm's Chapels, and their preservation is due to their being walled up during rebuilding operations. The 'St Paul of Malta', or, as it is sometimes called, 'St Paul and the Viper', is the most famous, the

Wall-painting at Claverley Church, Shropshire: Virtues and Vices in combat

St Paul at Malta: wall-painting from Canterbury Cathedral

best preserved and the finest painting from the twelfth century. There were schools of painting in some monastic establishments, and the better paintings, even in parish churches, must have been done under the inspiration of a monastic school; but this cannot have applied to all parish churches, where the village craftsman must sometimes have been called upon to do his simple best. The colours used depended on the locality and the wealth available. Black (which was carbon from charred wood or bones), white (which was lime) and red and yellow ochre were available to most, but the green, blue and vermilion were rarer. The green was probably malachite (green copper carbonate), and the blue, azurite (again copper carbonate). In spite of this some very fine paintings seem to have been produced with the more limited materials and 'green earth' was sometimes substituted for malachite, which is found only in Cornwall. More important than the artistic value of these paintings is the part that they all, good and bad alike, played in the lives of the people.

Henry III, in the thirteenth century, went in for mural decoration in a large way—painting, especially in green and gold, and wainscoting. But even in the twelfth century we get occasional glimpses of painted walls in domestic buildings. For instance, Henry II's chamber at Winchester was adorned with paintings, one of which, by special command of the king, showed a brood of four eaglets, preying on their parent and one of them perched on the neck ready to peck out the eyes. The painting was

162

allegorical. Henry's three eldest sons had already been involved
in treason against their father. His youngest and best beloved,
John, was to be involved in the final rebellion, which defeated
Henry and brought him in sorrow to the grave. The fourth
eaglet, poised to peck out the eyes of his parent, was indeed a
prophetic vision.

To return to the Church's problem of making its services intelligible to the laity, it became the custom in certain parts of
the liturgy to interpolate an explanatory phrase, called a trope.
The next step was to add mime and finally to introduce what was
in effect a short one-act play, with the priests as actors. Two
Church feasts were singled out for this treatment, the Nativity
and the Resurrection. The Nativity had a cycle which included
the Annunciation, the Visitation and the visits to the Babe at
Bethlehem. In one English 'drama' of the twelfth century the
kings were kings of Judah, indicating to the faithful the high
birth of Christ, an idea which was very palatable to the status-
conscious feudal nobility. The scene with the kings was often
played with a statue of the Virgin and Child on the altar behind a
curtain. Angels would draw the curtain to display the Infant
God. The kings would thereupon present their gifts and then
get into one bed, where the angel would appear, telling them to
go home by a different route. There were many possibilities in
the Easter cycle, but a favourite one was the discovery of the

*The three kings after their visit to the Babe at Bethlehem: a book illustration (c. 1180) of
a subject also popular in religious drama of the Christmas cycle*

Emmaus story: the artist attempts to depict movement in still pictures. (In the last, Christ is both rising from the table and disappearing through the door)

empty tomb. Another playlet, which originated in the twelfth century, was that of the meeting on the road to Emmaus, the supper at the inn and the vanishing of Christ. The stage directions say that Christ and the disciples are to wear pilgrim dress (*see* p. 96). These liturgical dramas had their counterparts in book illumination, where the illuminator did his best to get the effect of movement and drama in his somewhat limited medium.

Another artist treats Christ's disappearance differently

The theatreless public of the eleventh and twelfth centuries found the playlets good entertainment, and other subjects, which did not form part of the liturgy, began to receive the same treatment. The life of a saint, to celebrate his feast day, was an obvious choice. A particular episode from the life would be enacted, and enlivened with an entirely fictitious comic interlude. The play might be performed, not in the church but in front of the west door, so that the church itself formed the backcloth. St Paul's Church in London with its large open space, must have been a popular place for such a play, the audience standing round or

164

taking any point of vantage they could find.

Music is a natural outlet for man's feelings and spirits, so it must have played an important part in the life of any period, but before the thirteenth century the songs were mainly traditional and are lost to us. We have in early manuscripts drawings of musical instruments in quite a variety, horns, viols, zithers and harps in primitive forms. These were probably played in halls and palaces and their players may well have been regularly employed. Men did not travel alone if they could avoid it. Great men

Playing bells

travelled with their households and lesser folk would join forces for companionship and greater safety. Gerald of Wales tells us that Gilbert of Clare, travelling to his estates in Cardiganshire, was preceded by a minstrel and a singing man who played and sang alternately, and their noises alerted Gilbert's foes, the Welshmen who lay in ambush to kill him. Gerald says of the men of Yorkshire that 'where one voice is murmuring in the base, the other is warbling in the treble'. He attributes this to Danish influence. His native Welsh have as many different voices as there are heads in a crowd! The English, apparently, were wont to sing in unison.

Minstrel

For organised music, we turn again to the Church and particularly to the monasteries, where the Rule decreed many hours of liturgical singing each day. The chant used in England was the Gregorian, and the attempt of the Norman Abbot of Glastonbury to change it led to one of the great scandals of the Norman régime, the killing of some of the monks at the high altar by the Abbot's men-at-arms. A certain amount of polyphonic singing was introduced in the eleventh century, especially in the tropes, and the cloister children were used to combine treble with men's voices. There seems to have been a setback to this custom after the Conquest

165

Musicians

and, although it survived, it was not acceptable to all churchmen. We know that John of Salisbury found polyphony and variations in the liturgy unpleasing and that the saintly Cistercian, Ailred of Rievaulx, regretted that the common people were drawn to admire the sound of organs, the noise of cymbals and musical instruments, and harmony with pipes and cornets. He objected to the introduction of pleasure into the House of God. The organ to which Ailred objected was a pre-Conquest instrument. Duncan and Ethelwold, in the tenth century, had brought it into general monastic use. Tradition credits Ethelwold with building the Abingdon organ with his own hands. The one at St Swithin's, Winchester, was said to require 70 men to keep the pressure of air at its proper level. The resultant sound was apparently deafening in the small Anglo-Saxon churches. Improvements were made in the late eleventh century, so that the quality of the tone became sweeter. Organs were probably in general use, at any rate in the monastic churches, by the mid-twelfth century.

Juggling with balls or apples

The drama and music of the Church were didactic and devotional, but they also provided entertainment and gave pleasure. There were, however, other forms of entertainment which were purely secular. We have already mentioned the resident minstrels at the courts of kings and barons, including bishops. There were also

166

jesters and dancers and puppet shows. The founder of the Gilbertine order of canons and nuns, Gilbert of Sempringham, was, in his early days, mistaken for one of the Bishop of Lincoln's dancers (*saltatores*), when his gesticulations in his prayers in the church at night threw grotesque moving shadows on a lighted wall. These entertainers were completely reputable. Some of them were men of standing and some achieved considerable wealth. It was Rahere, Henry I's minstrel, who, in 1123, founded St Bartholomew's Priory and Hospital at Smithfield. Entertainers who had not the good fortune to be

Woman dancing

attached to a great household, or who preferred the open road like all true vagabonds, wandered from place to place, feast to feast, village to village or town to town. These were the less reputable members of the profession, and the minstrel who sang and accompanied himself on his vielle (a kind of fiddle) was not the only entertainer on the road. There were jugglers, acrobats, owners of performing bears and tellers of funny and often lewd stories. People welcomed them, but the Church denounced them. They were known as ribalds and lechers. Some of them were in fact monks or clerks who found the call of the tavern or the open road too strong for them. In the taverns they not only drank, but they diced. Gambling was a very old vice. Our Germanic ancestors would stake their wives or even their own freedom. That time was over, but it was still possible for the gambler to strip himself naked. As the Archpoet, one of these wandering clerks, though not an English one, sings in the midtwelfth century:

Twelfth-century puppet show

Performing bear

Yet a second charge they bring:
I'm for ever gaming.
Yea the dice hath many a time
Stripped me to my shaming.
What an if the body's cold
If the mind is burning.
On the anvil hammering
Rhymes and verses turning.

For on this my heart is set:
When the hour is nigh me,
Let me in the tavern die,
With a tankard by me,
While the angels looking down
Joyously sing o'er me
Deus sit propitius
Huic potatori.

Indoor games, possibly played in the chamber rather than the hall, seem to have changed little in two centuries. Chess and tables (a kind of backgammon) and dice predominate. According to Reginald of Durham there was a craftsman in Kirkcudbright in South Scotland, who made chessmen, draughts and dice out of walrus tusks and sold them.

The king set the fashion in outdoor sport, hunting with hounds and hawks, and all who had hunting rights or forests followed his example. Many of the tenants of the Bishop of Durham owed services in connection with his sport. Townsmen and countrymen alike enjoyed what sport they could, and poaching in royal and other forests must have been common, not only for the sport, but for its reward in the larder. Another sport, which was particularly popular among the younger members of the military caste, was miniature combat. It was a kind of free-for-all, with

Twelfth-century chessmen

168

knights charging in all directions over an undefined area. To bring this sport under control, so that it was not an occasion for rebellion, and, at the same time, to make it profitable to his exchequer, a matter ever near his heart, Richard I licensed the tournament in five special areas, all south of Yorkshire, and he imposed an entrance fee, ranging from 20 marks (£13 6s. 8d.) for an earl to two marks (£1 6s. 8d.) for a landless knight. According to FitzStephen, the young aspirants for knighthood were prepared to do mock battle with the sons of London's citizens, armed with lance and shield. Even younger lads joined in, armed with shafts forked at the end but with the iron tips removed.

London was a place of gaiety, and in the open fields outside the city there was ample room for wrestling, dancing and ball games, some of which seem to foreshadow our modern games. Easter time drew the people to the river and there were river sports, including an aquatic version of 'tilting at the quintain'. When the marshes north of London were flooded and frozen, winter sports would be in progress, with lumps of ice as sledges and animal shin-bones as skates. Accidents were frequent, but when has hot-blooded youth been deterred by such risks? Boar and bullbaiting for men and cockfighting for schoolboys were also common sports. All these are described by FitzStephen for London, but it is likely that most of them were countrywide.

It is perhaps not a bad thing that we should end this picture of life in Norman England on a note of gaiety. In spite of the conditions which

Twelfth-century ancestor of hockey and other modern ball games

would seem intolerable in the twentieth century, the various groups who together composed the population of England, did, each in its own way, enjoy life. The hardworking villeins, with their dark, smoky houses, enjoyed a periodic feast at their lord's expense, and although the lord's officials might be oppressive it was in their interest to see that the villein tenants had the wherewithal to keep their plots going. The manor was an integrated community. The conditions of living in the towns, except for the well-to-do, also left much to be desired, but the merchant and craft and other gilds looked after their members. Most churches took their duty of almsgiving seriously. Both the feudal community and the trading communities were, in a way, families and the relationship between members was much more intimate than is possible in a capitalist —or for that matter a communist—society. Monks and nuns either enjoyed their austerities, which is quite possible, or they enjoyed their backsliding. The aristocracy took itself very seriously, even in the matter of sport where jousting was regarded as a training for the aristocratic way of life, and hunting with hawks and hounds a twelfth-century way of 'keeping up with the Joneses'. It was only in their feasting that they really let themselves go. Probably the man who least enjoyed life in Norman England was the king, with his crushing burden of work and responsibility and his constant fear of treason and conspiracies. For him the hours spent in hunting were a well-earned relaxation.

Further Reading

D. Talbot Rice, *Oxford History of English Art, Vol. I: 871–1100*
T. S. R. Boase, *Oxford History of English Art, Vol. II: 1100–1216*
Eric Maclagan, *The Bayeux Tapestry* (King Penguin), 1943
E. W. Tristram, *English Medieval Wall Painting—the Twelfth Century*
Otto Pacht, *The Rise of Pictorial Narrative in Twelfth Century England*
E. K. Chambers, *The Medieval Stage* (2 vols.), 1903
J. Strutt, *The Sports and Pastimes of the People of England* (ed. Cox), 1903
H. J. R. Murry, *History of Chess* (2 vols.), 1952

Index

The numbers in heavy type refer to the pages on which illustrations appear

Pittance, pittancer, 95
Plagues, 56, 118, 119
Plough, ploughing, 13, 59, **60**, 82
Population, 6, 19, 78, 118
Portmanmoot (London Borough Court)
  83
Priests, 23, 49, 68, 76, 94, 100ff., **103**,
  132
Privies, 144
Property law, 132
Ptolemy, 115
Pullen, Robert, 106, 112
Punishments, 19, **109**, **128**, 130
Purbeck marble, 135, **136**

Quadripartitus, 125
Quadrivium, 110

Radbell the artificer, 136
Rahere (King's minstrel), 82, 167
Ralph, Earl, 2, 20, 22
Ralph of Diceto, 116
Ramsey Abbey, 75
Reading Abbey, 70, 147, **148**
'Realism', 110
Rectitudines Singularium Personarum,
  7, 10
Reeve, 59
Reginald of Durham, 106, 168
Renaissance, 2, 107
Ribbed vault, **98**, 134. **135**, **151**, **153**
Richard I, King, 1, 34, 38, 53
Richard le Poore, Bp of Salisbury, 72, 73
Richmond, Yorks., **52**
Rievaulx Abbey, 96, 154
Roads, 84, 127
Robert, son of William I, 35
Robert of Chester, 115
Robert of Gloucester, 124
Robert of Melun, 112
Rochester Castle, **35**
Roger, Archbp of York, 106
Roger, Bp of Salisbury, 19, 110
Roger of Hereford, 115
Roger of Montgomery, 57
*Roll of Ladies, Boys and Girls in the
  King's gift*, 53
Roman de Brut, 116
Romanesque architecture, 137
Romans, 114
Roofs, 140, **141**

Rouen, 72
Royal Chapel, 100

St Albans Abbey, 99, 106, 120
St Asaph's, 111
St Bartholomew's Priory and Hospital,
  London, 78, 167
St Edmund's Abbey, 21, 58, 71, 117,
  119, 129, 145, 149
St John's Chapel, 37
St Martin-le-Grand School, 79, 80
St Paul's, 58
  School, 79
St Peter's School, York, 105
St Stephen's Chapel, 37
Salerno medical school, 120
Salisbury, **73**, 107
  school at, 106
Salt, 18, 65, 66
Samson, Abbot of St Edmund's, 58, 61,
  106, 117
Samson, Bp of Worcester, 103, 105
Sanctuary, **131**
Sanitation, 80, 144
Schools, Chap. VI, 100
Science, 114
Sculptures, 138, 159
Scutage (shield money), 55
Selsey, Bp of, 23
Senlac Hill, 22
Serlo, Abbot of Gloucester, 88, 155
  candlestick of, **143**
Servants, 46
  royal, 42, 43
Services owed by the peasantry, 56, 57,
  59, 60
Sheep, shepherds, **9**, **65**, 75
Sherborne, Bp of, 23
Shipbuilding, 139, **140**
Shire reeve, *Scir-Gerefa* or Sheriff, 20
'Shots', 13
Shrewsbury, 73
Shropshire, 35
Simeon, Prior of Winchester, 94
Siward, Earl of Northumbria, 20
Skating, 169
Slaves, 7, 11, 57
Smith, **7**, 13, 145, **147**
Smithfield Market, 60, 78, 167
Song of Roland, 116
Soulscot (burial fees), 67

176